FREIGHTERS

Antonov 124s do it, Boeing 747s do it, even ATRs do it, they all serve as freighters, aircraft that carry cargo in bulk.

Cargolux, DHL, FedEx and UPS are some of the world's most instantly recognised airlines. But none of them carry any passengers. And, in the age of modern global trading, these commercial cargo airlines make the world go around. Not to be outdone by commercial operators, one of the largest air cargo handlers is the US Air Force Air Mobility Command. Its Aerial Ports oversee tens of thousands of tons of cargo and material each year. That cargo is managed by aerial port squadrons, the biggest of which is the 436th based

at Dover Air Force Base, Delaware. Co-located with the 436th Airlift Wing we tell their joint story.

In the commercial world we take an extensive look at Luxembourg-based Cargolux and its fleet of Boeing 747-8 freighters, DHL's operation based at East Midlands Airport in the UK, and those of United Parcel Service Airline. All fascinating companies with interesting stories.

Whether under commercial or military ownership, all cargo carriers require a cargo network, aerial ports, aircraft, aircrew, load crews and cargo handling equipment, to name but a few of the basics.

Such iconic aircraft as the Airbus A330, Antonov An-124, Boeing 747, Lockheed C-5 Galaxy and the McDonnell-Douglas

MD-11 serve as freighters. Over 2,000 aircraft are in operation as commercially owned freighters, with hundreds more assigned to military air arms. Freighter aircraft deliver stuff all over the world. Much of that stuff is essential to daily life, from vegetables to soap, from coffee to pharmaceuticals.

It's a fascinating operation and whatever your interest in aviation, *Freighters - Air Cargo Kings* provides a detailed insight to the world of freight aviation.

Mark Ayton

Mark Ayton
Editor

(Eviation)

CONTENTS

(US Air Force) AIR MOBILITY COMMAND 18

(Israel Aerospace Industries)

(Boeing)

(ATR)

ISBN: 978 1 80282 744 6
Editor: Mark Ayton
Senior editor, specials: Roger Mortimer
Email: roger.mortimer@keypublishing.com
Cover design: Dan Jarman
Design: SJmagic DESIGN SERVICES, India
Advertising Sales Manager: Brodie Baxter
Email: brodie.baxter@keypublishing.com
Tel: 01780 755131
Advertising Production: Debi McGowan
Email: debi.mcgowan@keypublishing.com

SUBSCRIPTION/MAIL ORDER
Key Publishing Ltd, PO Box 300, Stamford, Lincs, PE9 1NA
Tel: 01780 480404
Subscriptions email: subs@keypublishing.com

Mail Order email: orders@keypublishing.com
Website: www.keypublishing.com/shop

PUBLISHING
Group CEO: Adrian Cox
Publisher, Books and Bookazines: Jonathan Jackson
Published by
Key Publishing Ltd, PO Box 100, Stamford, Lincs, PE9 1XQ
Tel: 01780 755131 **Website:** www.keypublishing.com

PRINTING
Precision Colour Printing Ltd, Haldane, Halesfield 1, Telford, Shropshire. TF7 4QQ

DISTRIBUTION
Seymour Distribution Ltd, 2 Poultry Avenue, London, EC1A 9PU
Enquiries Line: 02074 294000.

Off the Shelves

N7901A

A look at the air cargo market and how digitalisation and sustainability are affecting the sector.

In early 2020 the global logistics market saw huge and rapid growth thanks to the urgent requirement to move medical supplies to cope with the COVID-19 pandemic, and surging e-commerce demand as consumer shopping habits changed.

During a June 2021 webinar Henk Mulder, the International Air Transport Association (IATA) head of digital cargo, observed that the sector experienced the equivalent of three years' growth in a single year (2020-2021).

The greater demand increased pressure on the major shipping companies moving goods worldwide. As IATA noted in its September 2021 air cargo market update: "Strong demand for

goods, combined with COVID-19 control measures, has disrupted production at manufacturers."

It continued: "As there is not enough capacity for shipments on most modes of transport, this translates into long delivery times and delays. Key inputs such as semiconductors are difficult to get, meaning there is a second impact on goods that use them, such as phones."

Eyes to the skies

Ocean-going shipping is set for growth long term. A December 2021 forecast by the New York-based consultancy Market Research Future predicted the market will be worth $22bn by 2030.

Supply-chain bottlenecks right now, however, mean the main cargo shippers – including AP Moller-Maersk, CMA CGM, DB Schenker, Evergreen, Hapag-Lloyd, MSC Mediterranean Shipping Company and Nippon Express – need capacity and the ability to transport goods quickly.

Shippers have increasingly looked skywards for the answer. In November 2021, Bloomberg quoted Freightos, which operates the WebCargo bookings platform, as reporting that air cargo demand jumped by more than 1,000% year-on-year during 2020-2021.

A consequence of higher air cargo demand is some shippers seeking to strengthen their own presence in the arena, rather

Amazon Prime Air Boeing 737-800(BCF) freighter on approach to New York-JFK Airport operated as Sun Country Flight SY3054. Sun Country Airlines is the contract operator for the airframe, which utilises airframes leased by Amazon from GE Capital. (Wikipedia/Adam Moreira)

than relying on capacity provided by partners or established cargo airlines.

In November 2021, the world's largest shipping line, the Danish company AP Moller-Maersk, announced a major expansion to its air capacity. Another shipper, CMA CGM Group, launched a dedicated airline unit in March 2021, with four Airbus A330-200Fs operated by Air Belgium.

On November 2, 2021, Boeing, and A.P. Moller - Maersk (Maersk) announced an order for two 777 Freighters to be operated by Star Air, Maersk's in-house aircraft operator. At the time of the order, Star Air operated an all-Boeing 767 freighter fleet.

Vincent Clerc, executive vice president and CEO of Ocean & Logistics,

A.P. Moller – Maersk said: "As a global integrator of container logistics, Maersk is improving the ability to provide one-stop shop and end-to-end logistics capabilities to our customers. This year, we have strengthened our integrated logistics offering through e-commerce logistics acquisitions, tech investments, expanding our warehouse footprint and as a natural next step, we are now ramping up our air freight capacity, creating a broader network to cater even better for the needs of customers."

Blurred Lines

Major shipping companies such as CMA CGM and Maersk expanding capacity

is not the only ripple in the air cargo market caused by COVID-19.

Lionel van der Walt, chief commercial officer of PayCargo – a financial technology specialist that offers payment transfer services for cargo companies – said the pandemic had fundamentally shifted the structure of the freight industry.

Air Cargo Expansion at Maersk

In November 2021, AP Moller-Maersk announced the intended acquisition of Senator International – a German freight-forwarding company with a presence in 21 countries across Europe, the Americas and Asia. The acquisition was completed on June 2, 2022.

Maersk, the global provider of end-to-end container logistics placed
an order for two Boeing 777 Freighters for operation by Star Air,
Maersk's in-house aircraft operator on November 2, 2021. (Boeing)

Senator has a well-developed airfreight network comprising own controlled flights and long-term partnerships with best-in-class airlines, a well-established full container load and less than container load network and specialised services such as packaging, warehousing, and distribution across five continents. The acquisition enables Maersk to offer a wider range of products and the ability to provide flexible and integrated logistics solutions to its customers, allowing them to speed up or slow down cargo depending on their changing supply chain needs.

Following the acquisition, Clerc said: "We are delighted to welcome the Senator team to our Maersk family. As a global provider of integrated logistics, we are improving our ability to provide end-to-end solutions to our customers. With Senator on board, we are ramping up our air freight capacity, network, and know-how significantly to cater even better for our customers."

At the same time, Boeing announced that Maersk had placed an order for two 777 Freighters for operation by its in-house aircraft operator, Star Air, now Maersk Air Cargo.

In a Boeing statement, Clerc is quoted as saying: "As a global integrator of container logistics, Maersk is improving the ability to provide one-stop shop and end-to-end logistics capabilities to our customers. This year, we have strengthened our integrated logistics offering through e-commerce logistics acquisitions, tech investments, expanding our warehouse footprint and as a natural next step, we are now ramping up our air freight capacity, creating a broader network to cater even better for the needs of customers."

A Maersk statement said: "Maersk's ambition is to have approximately one-third of its annual air tonnage carried within its own controlled freight network. This will be achieved through a combination of owned and leased aircraft, replicating the structure that the company has within its ocean fleet. The remaining capacity will be provided by strategic commercial carriers and charter flight operators."

Speaking during the June 2021 IATA webinar on digital cargo, van der Walt explained that, historically, the cargo ecosystem has maritime vendors (ocean carriers and ports), aviation vendors (airlines and airports), rail and road vendors, and what PayCargo calls 'payers' (shippers, freight forwarders and brokers).

According to van der Walt, COVID-19 blurred the traditional lines between these different parties. He said: "We've seen a lot of payers starting to realise they can pay other payers, and at the same time we've seen what we consider traditional vendors also realise there's value in using paid cargo. We've ended up with an ecosystem where all the users can be considered both vendors and payers."

A rendering of an Eviation Alice eCargo aircraft –a fully electric platform with 440nm range and 2,600lb payload capacity in the colours of DHL Express. (Eviation)

The shift has occurred at the same time as end customers' demands for speedy deliveries have grown considerably. Van der Walt feels "the freight industry needs to rely on advanced technologies to keep pace" with greater expectations. He warned: "Failure to adopt [new] solutions will be costly and lead to significant disruptions."

Van der Walt believes the importance of embracing new technology is underlined by major shipping companies increasing their air cargo presence. With the shippers having a large presence in road, rail, and sea transport, they will "need to take systems and make things seamless across their business, so they cross the modes."

On April 8, 2022, Maersk launched Maersk Air Cargo and chose Denmark's second largest airport, Billund, as its air freight hub. The company now operates daily flights from Billund.

Existing in-house aircraft operator, Star Air, has transferred its activities into Maersk Air Cargo, with the new carrier supporting existing and new customers and Maersk's end to end logistics.

Aymeric Chandavoine, Global Head of Logistics and Services, A.P. Moller – Maersk said: "Air freight is a crucial enabler of flexibility and agility in global supply chains as it allows our customers to tackle time-critical supply chain challenges and provides transport mode options for high value cargo. We strongly believe in working closely with our customers. Therefore, it is key for Maersk to also increase our presence in the global air cargo industry by introducing Maersk Air Cargo to cater even better for the needs of our customers."

Maersk Air Cargo currently operates a fleet of 17 Boeing 767-200 and 767-300 freighter aircraft. Two new Boeing 777Fs are expected to be operational in 2024.

Maersk's ambition is to have approximately one third of its annual air tonnage carried within its own controlled freight network. This is being achieved through a combination of owned and leased aircraft, replicating the structure that the company has within its ocean fleet. The remaining capacity will be provided by strategic commercial carriers and charter flight operators.

Cargo Evolves

This bigger picture means digitalisation is one of the most important aspects of the current air cargo market, and Frankfurt based Lufthansa Cargo provides an example of how airfreight specialists are responding to the arrival of new technologies.

During the June 2021 IATA digital cargo webinar, Lufthansa Cargo's CEO Dorothea von Boxberg highlighted three of the company's digital initiatives: e-Booking, e-Freight, and PreCheck.

The e-Booking capability uses digital data exchange to create faster and simpler booking for flights. The company has its own interface that shows 24/7 updates on bookable prices/slots, flight plans and calculations on carbon dioxide emissions from the flights. There is also access to WebCargo and cargo.one - another booking portal.

Von Boxberg said Lufthansa Cargo customers can "book air cargo capacities across multiple airlines within seconds," adding: "My idea is always 'let the customer go where it's most convenient'. It's their choice, that's why we're open to other platforms."

A second project is e-Freight. This is an industry-wide initiative involving cargo carriers, freight forwarders, ground handlers, shippers, customs brokers, and customs authorities to, IATA says, "build an end-to-end paperless transportation process for air cargo, through a regulatory framework, electronic messages and high data quality".

IATA's e-Freight roadmap involves digitising customs documents and procedures, starting with the introduction of an electronic Air Waybill (eAWB). An Air Waybill is the critical air cargo document that constitutes the contract of carriage between a shipper and carrier (airline).

In January, 2019 IATA's Electronic Air Waybill Resolution 672 removed the requirement for a paper AWB, meaning eAWB became the default contract of carriage for all air cargo shipments. The association describes it as a milestone for air cargo, "where digital processes are now the norm and paper is the exception."

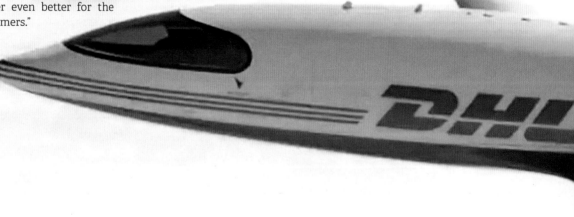

Von Boxberg said Lufthansa Cargo was working to achieve 100% eAWB usage across its business by the end of 2022 and for shipments that are not delivered as eAWB, Lufthansa Cargo now applies a chargeable 'Paper-to-eAWB' (P2e) service which enables a paper- to an eAWB shipment. She noted some further work was required to finalise the aspects of eAWB related to dangerous goods declarations.

Another aspect of Lufthansa Cargo's digitalisation efforts is PreCheck, which involves introducing new services for paperless freight and documentation that enable acceptance of cargo 'off airport', prior to delivery, so there is a faster handover of shipments at the airport. PreCheck also includes 24/7 data support.

Amazon Air

Amazon Air provides another interesting example of the air cargo sector's evolution. Launched in 2016 (it was known as Amazon Prime Air for its first year), Amazon Air has expanded quickly. The company has regional hubs at Fort Worth Alliance Airport, Texas, Cincinnati/Northern Kentucky International Airport and San Bernadino Airport, California, and operates a dense network of point-to-point services across the United States. The company also operates services from Leipzig/Halle Airport, Germany.

Amazon Air has grown its presence by wet leasing aircraft from specialist cargo carriers, with Amazon-branded Boeing 737s and 767s operated by Atlas Air, Air Transport Services Group, ASL Airlines Ireland, Silver Airways, Southern Air and Sun Country Airlines.

According to a March 2023 fleet listing on planespotters.net, Amazon Air now has 91 aircraft, comprising 56 767-300Fs, 30 737-800BCFs (Boeing Converted Freighters) and five ATR 72s.

Amazon did not respond to questions about Amazon Air and its plans for the unit but, on the 767 acquisition, Sarah Rhoads, vice president of Amazon Global Air, said: "Having a mix of both leased and owned aircraft in our growing fleet allows us to better manage our operations, which in turn helps us to keep pace in meeting our customer promises."

Separately, in May 2021, Amazon announced an investment – through its Climate Pledge Fund – in BETA Technologies, the US start-up developing the striking Alia electric vertical take-off and landing aircraft designed to carry three cargo pallets.

In a statement, Amazon vice president and head of worldwide sustainability Kara Hurst said: "We support BETA Technologies' mission to reshape air transportation through zero-emission aviation and are proud to invest in them."

Using Data

Van der Walt thinks a key aspect of digitalisation in air cargo is using data intelligently. He stated that PayCargo, "at its core, is facilitating payments, but the way we do this is to focus on ensuring a seamless flow of data across systems and then providing instant access, so people have visibility about what is transpiring across the business."

PayCargo does more than just present data – its users have active control of some processes that affect their operations, such as facilitating payments or managing who can authorise them, and it offers customised workflows and functionalities.

"The integrations we do, both with vendors and payers, are critical to the value that it adds to both sides of the equation," van der Walt said. "It really helps to eliminate a lot of manual processes [and] having to access multiple systems."

Riege Software produces operating software for the documentation that enables logistics companies, freight forwarders and handling/customs agents to move cargo from place to place.

Christian Riege, the company's managing director and senior vice-president software development, believes there is an opportunity for the cargo industry to use the increased focus on digitalisation to revolutionise processes.

During a July 2021 IATA webinar, Riege drew a comparison with passenger air transport – where digital technology has

DHL Express has ordered 12 Eviation Alice eCargo fully electric aircraft for delivery from 2024. (Eviation)

brought global commonality in tickets, boarding passes, and processes. "It's the same code that's in the central systems that keep the data," he noted, enabling travellers to print and scan their own tickets and undertake self-check-in worldwide.

In comparison, Riege said: "Cargo cannot speak, listen, read, react, or complain, take care of accompanying documents, [and] change aircraft and places when required. We have multiple stakeholders and participants [and] multiple IT systems, each suited to its own niche of the supply chain – the shipper, the freight forwarder, ground handlers, customs agents, airlines.

"They all need to talk to each other. We need one IT system with one technical [meta] language to share the data. Cargo needs its own language that is universally understood." Riege has urged the sector to invest in automation, to bring about technical interoperability – his presentation noted "willingness, involvement [and] collaboration" are required to achieve it.

ONE Record

The e-Freight project and eAWB are clearly steps forward for interoperability – and another is IATA's ONE Record.

This is a standard structure for data exchange that, IATA explained, "creates a single record view of the shipment" by defining a common data model. The standard uses what the agency calls "mature but progressive data-sharing technologies that are well aligned with the best practices used by leading airlines."

It is based on what IATA calls "an industrywide and federated trust network to manage identification and authentication of data-sharing systems and ensures data privacy and confidentiality for all parties."

The agency said: "The objective of ONE Record is to address the main challenges of e-Freight, unlock the possibilities of a full digital air cargo industry and create opportunities for new value-added services and business models."

IATA stated ONE Record will improve data quality and control, visibility, and transparency for the entire transportation chain, and offer 'plug and play' connectivity through its application programming interface.

On its website, IATA states: "ONE Record creates the foundation for true digital air cargo, where airlines, their partners and service providers will be able to develop collaborative and automated digital services.

"ONE Record provides a technology platform that is ready for a new generation of digital natives who will be leading the logistics and transport industry within a decade."

Riege Software is contributing its Cargo XML conversion toolkit to IATA's Digital Cargo working group that is steering the work on ONE Record.

Sustainability

Alongside digitalisation, another big issue on the agenda for the air cargo sector is sustainability – just as it is for numerous other industries.

During the IATA webinar, Lufthansa Cargo's von Boxberg disclosed that sustainability is "the most discussed topic in all the customer meetings I've had. It's a topic that's really taken [off] considerably."

Digitalisation could contribute to the sector's sustainability efforts. Riege noted the company's software can be used by customers to track CO_2 emissions from their shipments, and Lufthansa Cargo customers can use a calculator on its website to track CO_2 emissions of their flight.

Lufthansa Cargo now solely operates newer, more fuel-efficient Boeing 777Fs, after phasing out its last Boeing MD-11F in October 2022. It uses new lightweight containers to reduce aircraft weight and lower fuel burn, and it has also used sustainable aviation fuels for some of its flights.

Early in 2022, the company introduced AeroSHARK on its 777Fs. Developed by sister company Lufthansa Technik, AeroSHARK is a durable bionic film applied to specific parts of an aircraft. It mimics sharkskin, to optimise airflow around the fuselage, so the aircraft flies more efficiently and uses less fuel.

The film – manufactured by chemicals and coatings specialist BASF – is sized in patches for easy and targeted application. Each piece contains millions of prism-shaped, 50µm-high 'riblets' that are aligned to the airflow. The film is designed to be resilient and to withstand the large temperature and pressure differentials, as well as the ultraviolet radiation, encountered during high-altitude flight.

Lufthansa Cargo says AeroSHARK will generate annual savings of about 3,700 tons of kerosene and about 11,500 tons of CO_2 emissions for its 777Fs.

New Freighters

With sustainability becoming a focus, unsurprisingly there have been orders for newer, less-polluting aircraft.

An artist rendering of a fully electric Eviation Alice eCargo freighter aircraft. (Eviation)

Recent announcements include DHL Express ordering 12 Eviation Alice eCargo aircraft – a fully electric platform with 440nm (815km) range and 2,600lb (5,732kg) payload capacity – for delivery from 2024.

Both CMA CGM and the lessor Air Lease have ordered Airbus's recently launched A350 Freighter, which the manufacturer claims will burn 40% less fuel and emit 40% fewer CO_2 emissions than the Boeing 747F, while offering the same cargo volume. Boeing offers the 777-8F as a rival to the new Airbus model.

Pandemic Air Cargo in Figures

Speaking in October 2021, Brendan Sullivan, IATA's global head of cargo, said: "During the crisis, air cargo has been a lifeline for society, delivering critical medical supplies and vaccines across the globe and keeping international supply chains open. In 2020, the air cargo industry generated $129bn, which represented approximately a third of airlines' overall revenues, an increase of 10-15% compared to pre-crisis levels."

IATA's latest air cargo figures, released in December 2022 and covering October 2022, show global demand, measured in cargo weight and distance, was down 8.0% compared to October 2021. IATA notes: "Available cargo tonne-kilometres (ACTKs) contracted by 2.2% year-on-year [YoY] in December 2022 – the third month in a row of YoY contractions. This is mainly a result of airlines responding to supply imbalances from the softening demand. Compared to December 2019, North America continued to be

the only region fully recovered to pre-pandemic levels in terms of total CTKs. Latin America sustained its lead in the growth of international CTKs among all regions, registering a 2.3% YoY growth in December. Inflation in the G7 countries pulled back to 6.8% in December from 7.4% in November - the greatest decline in 2022. Both oil and jet fuel prices declined in December, slightly decreasing the unusually wide jet crack spread."

The boom in air cargo demand has led to orders for converted freighters, both smaller A320 and 737-sized jets and the various 767 and 777 conversions.

On November 15, 2021, during the Dubai airshow, Airbus announced that Air Lease Corporation had signed a Letter of Intent for 25 A220-300s, 55 A321neos, 20 A321XLRs, four A330neos and seven A350 Freighters. The order made the Los Angeles based ALC the launch customer and lessor for the A350F.

The A350F is optimised for cargo operations offering at least 20% lower fuel burn than the competition and the only new generation freighter aircraft ready for the 2027 ICAO CO_2 emissions standards.

Hot on the heels of the Airbus announcement, on January 31, 2022, Boeing launched the new 777-8 Freighter with a firm order for 34 jets and options for 16 from Qatar Airways. Boeing said: "Featuring advanced technology from the new 777X family and the proven performance of the 777 Freighter, the 777-8 Freighter will be the largest, longest-range and most capable twin-engine freighter in the industry. With payload capacity nearly identical to the 747-400 Freighter and a 25% improvement in fuel efficiency, emissions, and operating costs, the 777-8 Freighter will enable a more sustainable and profitable business for operators.

An artist rendering of boxes being loaded into the cargo hold of an Eviation Alice eCargo freighter aircraft. (Eviation)

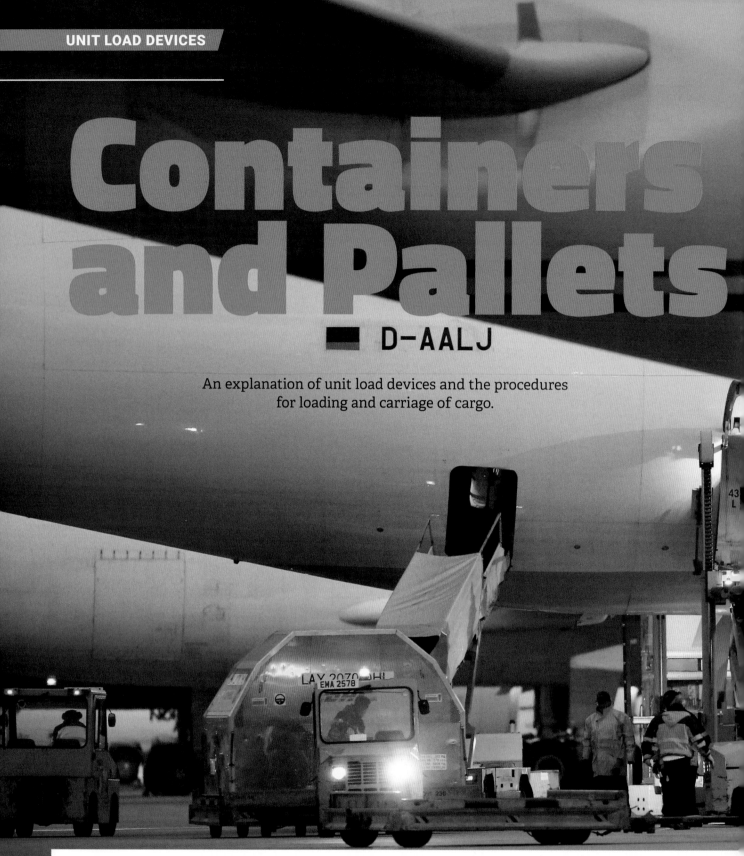

Containers and Pallets

■ D-AALJ

An explanation of unit load devices and the procedures
for loading and carriage of cargo.

A ccording to the International
Air Transport Association
(IATA) a unit load device
(ULD) is either an aircraft
pallet and pallet net
combination, or an aircraft container.

ULDs are removable aircraft parts
subject to strict civil aviation authorities'
requirements from design, testing,
production, and operations, to repair and
maintenance. An airworthy ULD must
be structurally capable of restraining the
loads and providing adequate protection

to the aircraft systems and structure
during flight.

ULDs are the only aircraft parts that
leave the control of the airline, return after
passing through many unregulated hands,
and have an impact on flight safety. As
most ULD operations are outsourced to
ground service providers, together with the
increasing demands for shipper-built ULDs
from shippers and freight forwarders,
it has become critically challenging for
airlines to control and supervise the safety
compliance in ULD operations.

Unit Load Device

ULDs are divided into two types: Pallets
and containers.

Pallets are secured by a net, attached
to the rim of the pallet. The final shape
(contour) chosen in the build-up of a
ULD needs to fit the allocated aircraft
type. Pallets are used if the cargo is
difficult to fit into containers, if there
are more options for build-up, or when
a pallet is the only way to carry special
load cargo.

6-DDA

(East Midlands Airport)

LAK 1313 DHL

AMX 9708 DHL

ALP 0702 DHL   ALP 0

The alternative to a pallet is a container which provides the shape (contour). The contents are secured either by closing and bolting the doors, or by securing the door net to the rims of the container walls and floor. A container is faster to load/unload than a pallet and provides the cargo with better protection against damage and weather conditions.

In general, ULDs are owned by airlines so the respective handling agents must maintain a regular stock check. Both the airline and its agent must complete a UCR

(ULD Control Receipt) when releasing or accepting ULDs: a vital document for determining responsibility and liability for the release and acceptance process.

Contours (the overall shape) are created for the build-up of open pallet ULDs with consideration and adherence given to the routing, the type of recipient aircraft, and its loading position on that aircraft.

ULD contours take account of the structural dimensions of the recipient aircraft to be loaded.

Standard form ULDs tend to fit on most types of aircraft and in most positions, other types of aircraft require non-standard sized ULDs, especially for specific positions, with the correct contour. Before build-up begins, the maximum loading capacity of the aircraft type and the ULD must be confirmed.

For cargo that requires special handling, both the handling agent and the airline must take precautions that protect the cargo, the aircraft, handling personnel, and accompanying

(Lufthansa)

consignments. Priority handling is necessary for urgent cargo.

Tie-Down

When securing cargo loaded on a pallet, the base is covered with plastic sheeting, and the load shaped to the correct contour for its loading position on the aircraft. A plastic sheet is used to cover the load and give protection against the elements. The net used to secure the load is checked for serviceability and placed over the consignment covering all packages.

Before tensioning the net, fittings are attached and evenly spread out. Corner lashings tighten the load down in accordance with the contents: straps should be tensioned without damaging the cargo or bending the pallet.

A serviceable net used on the main cargo deck must withstand a 15,000lb loading.

When placing cargo in a container it has to be loaded in a way that it will not fall out when the door is open. Containers fitted with a flexible door must be loaded in a way that avoids the packages pressing against the plastic door or deforming the container's contour.

Additional tie downs, lashing or strapping may be required for special loads or unusual consignments such as aircraft engines, cars, and some machinery, dependent on its weight and the capacity of the tie downs, lashing and strapping being used.

Tie down attachment points must be spaced evenly to allow maximum effectiveness, at a minimum 10in from the corner of the pallet.

By spreading the weight of the load over as much of the surface area available in a pallet or container it's more secure and facilitates easier loading, an even weight

and balance of the aircraft, and avoids damaging the aircraft's structure.

Identification

Once a ULD is built-up and complete to make it available and acceptable for loading onto the aircraft must have a ULD tag listing all the information required by ramp agents. Before loading onto the aircraft, the information is cross-referenced with the flight documentation.

To load the aircraft correctly, the ULD tag must list the following information: correct tag for the consignments loaded on/in the ULD; a ULD number; its destination, gross weight and airline, and a signature stating the ULD is correctly built and the weight correctly established.

The ramp agent must then ensure the ULD is not overweight for its loading position on the aircraft position and is within the maximum gross weight for the type of ULD.

The tag is affixed on the long side of the pallet by wire fasteners or in a pocket on container door to ease the information cross-checking, a process completed before being unloaded from the K-loader or truck. A discrepancy can deem the

ULD non-compliant for loading such that it has to be returned to the handling company for rectification.

Aircraft Characteristics

The primary types of aircraft that carry ULDs are those classed as wide-body and freighters.

Wide Bodied aircraft have a forward and an aft hold in the lower deck which are divided into compartments that accommodate ULDs.

Freighters carry cargo in the lower and main decks providing capacity for large consignments, larger quantities, and with fewer restrictions for dangerous goods.

All aircraft have maximum weight limits for each loading position, compartment, and hold. The IATA issue a guide to the many sizes and specifications in common use, several of them are included here along with their designations, sizes, restrictions, and suitability in terms of the aircraft they can be carried on.

Dangerous Goods

Commodities that possess potentially hazardous characteristics are deemed as dangerous goods and require stringent precautions for transportation onboard an aircraft. Dangerous goods range from acids, through radioactive materials, to aerosol sprays, and bleach.

Technical instructions for the safe transportation of dangerous goods by aircraft issued by IATA contain internationally agreed rules and the procedures that must be followed by all personnel involved for preparing each consignment and loading it/them on an aircraft.

Dangerous goods are divided into four categories: acceptable, forbidden, forbidden but exempted by those states involved in the flight plan, and excepted.

ULD loading facts

- ULDs are loaded on ball mat, not on the floor.
- All shipments loaded on or in a ULD must be destined for the same offloading station.
- All pieces belonging to one shipment should be loaded on or into the same ULD where possible.
- Large or heavy pieces are loaded on pallets, small pieces are best loaded in containers.
- Heavy or sturdy pieces are loaded as a first or bottom layer.
- Light pieces are then loaded on top to lessen the chance of damage.
- Wooden pallets, supporting platforms or planks are used for loading pieces with a metal base to prevent the piece slipping whilst in transit. Additional lashing may be required.

MAIL ORDER

Eagle Wing

Mark Ayton details military operations with the 436th Airlift Wing and the 436th Aerial Port Squadron.

A 436th Aerial Port Squadron ramp services supervisor, positions a cargo loader at the rear of a C-5M Super Galaxy at Dover Air Force Base, Delaware. The cargo shown is owned by the US Navy's Supervisor of Salvage and Diving. (US Air Force/Roland Balik)

Cargo processors secure a pallet at the aerial port on Dover Air Force Base. Each pallet-building station lowers for improved ergonomics and safety. (US Air Force/Senior Airman Aaron Jenne)

D over Air Force Base is home to the US Department of Defense's largest aerial port and nearly 9,000 airmen and joint service members, civilians, and families. Personnel at the Kent County, Delaware, complex are responsible for global airlift aboard C-5M Super Galaxy and C-17 Globemaster III aircraft assigned to the resident 436th Airlift Wing. The C-5Ms are operated by the 9th Airlift Squadron, the C-17As by the 3rd Airlift Squadron.

According to Air Mobility Command: "The C-5M and C-17A together comprise our strategic airlift fleet, which together allow us to project decisive strength and deliver hope, sustainability and lethality to the right place at the right time. The C-5 fleet of 52 aircraft provides unmatched airlift capability as the largest aircraft in the US Air Force inventory, and its primary mission is to airlift combat forces, equipment, and supplies. Our 222-strong C-17 fleet combines tactical capability with strategic range and is capable of rapid strategic delivery of troops and all types of cargo to main operating

bases or agile combat employment directly to austere airfield environments."

Additionally, the 436th hosts key partners, such as the Air Force Reserve's 512th Airlift Wing, Air Force Mortuary Affairs Operations (AFMAO), the Armed Forces Medical Examiner System (AFMES) and the Joint Personal Effects Depot (JPED), jointly responsible for the dignified return of fallen American service members.

Known as the Eagle Wing, the 436th comprises more than 4,000 active-duty airmen and answers to the 18th Air Force and Air Mobility Command, both located at Scott Air Force Base, Illinois.

One of the wing's most significant component units is the 436th Aerial Port Squadron known as the 'Super Port'. The 436th APS has the greatest material handling capability, the propensity of air transportation manning and the most extensive facilities. It is the prime mover of passengers and cargo throughout

multiple combatant commands to support operations directed by the President of the United States, the Department of Defense, or the Joint Chiefs of Staff, as well as United Nations peacekeeping efforts worldwide.

The 512th Airlift Wing, also known as Liberty Wing, is an Air Force Reserve unit assigned to Dover Air Force Base and assists with maintenance and operation of the C-5M and C-17A aircraft assigned to the 436th AW; the C-5Ms of the 709th Airlift Squadron and the C-17As of the 326th Airlift Squadron.

Combined, the two wings fly hundreds of missions throughout the world, providing movement of outsized and oversized cargo, and personnel on scheduled, special assignment, exercise, and contingency airlift missions. Together, they account for 20% of the nation's strategic outsized airlift capability, projecting global reach to more than 100 countries.

Outsized cargo is defined as cargo that won't fit on a single aircraft pallet. Oversized cargo is cargo that, due to its size and dimensions, requires marrying together over multiple pallets for loading. Examples include large, rolling stock items such as tanks and helicopters, or any type of load that requires special tie-down and centre-of-balance markings.

Air Force Mortuary Affairs Operations (AFMAO) is charged with fulfilling the USA's commitment of ensuring dignity, honour, and respect to the fallen. It ensures that a solemn, dignified transfer of remains from the aircraft to a transfer

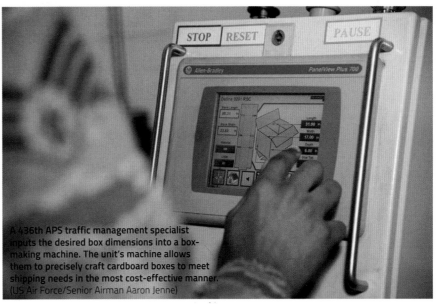

A 436th APS traffic management specialist inputs the desired box dimensions into a box-making machine. The unit's machine allows them to precisely craft cardboard boxes to meet shipping needs in the most cost-effective manner. (US Air Force/Senior Airman Aaron Jenne)

A ramp supervisor assigned to the 436th Aerial Port Squadron, marshals a Humvee down the forward loading ramp of a C-5M Super Galaxy at Dover Air Force Base, Delaware. (US Air Force/ Roland Balik)

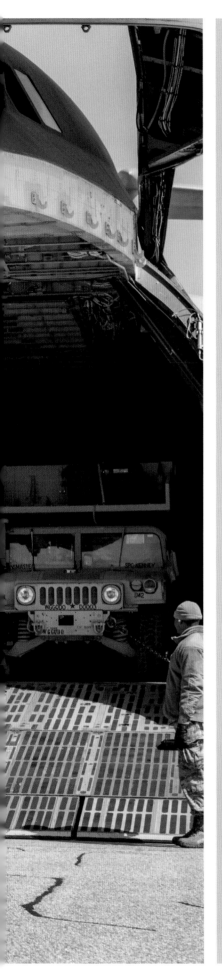

C-5M Super Galaxy

A modernised version of the legacy C-5 strategic transport aircraft designed and manufactured by Lockheed Martin. It is the largest aircraft in the US Air Force inventory with a 100ft long, 17ft 2in wide and 13ft 6in high cargo compartment with front and rear access doors. Its primary mission is transportation of cargo, outsized cargo, and personnel for the Department of Defense, usually over intercontinental ranges.

Thanks to the front and rear access doors, load teams can simultaneously load and offload cargo from both ends, reducing transfer times. Full-width drive-on ramps at each end of the aircraft enable double rows of vehicles to be transported.

Undertaken between 2002 and 2012, the Avionics Modernization Program (AMP) provided 27 C-5As (since retired), 50 C-5Bs and two C-5Cs with updated digital flight decks.

The AMP was followed by the Reliability Enhancement and Reengining Program (RERP) which involved replacement of the C-5's original General Electric TF39 turbofans with General Electric F138-GE-100 (CF6-80C2) engines. In addition to improving fuel consumption, the F138 delivers a 22% increase in power.

RERP also incorporated more than 50 improvements to the Galaxy's structure and systems that included a new auxiliary power unit and a Large Aircraft Infra-Red Countermeasures (LAIRCM) system.

One C-5A, two C-5Cs and 49 C-5B aircraft were modified with the RERP and assigned the C-5M designation.

The two C-5Cs were originally modified to transport US Air Force and NASA space programme cargo. After the RERP modifications were completed on the two C-5C aircraft they are referred to as C-5M Space Cargo Modified (SCM) aircraft.

The RERP started in 2006 and completed 12 years later when Lockheed Martin delivered the final C-5M to the US Air Force on August 2, 2018.

The US Air Force's FY2021 budget provided over $50m for avionics-related upgrades for the C-5M fleet. A Communication Navigation Surveillance/Air Traffic Management (CNS/ATM) upgrade includes Automatic Dependent Surveillance-Broadcast Out (ADS-B Out) capability, identification friend or foe (IFF) mode 5, and replacement of the aircraft's satellite communication equipment and beyond line-of-sight voice radio.

The Core Mission Computer/Weather Radar (CMC/WxR) upgrade is designed to provide a new Core Mission Computer (CMC) and the Collins Aerospace WXR-2100 weather radar and serves as the baseline for all future C-5M modifications.

On June 2, 2022, Lockheed Martin was awarded a $34.7m contract modification for the C-5M Replacement Multi-Functional Control Display Program. This contract modification provides for engineering and technical services to produce a hardware and software prototype architecture for transition into the engineering and manufacturing development phase. Performed in Fort Worth, Texas, the prototyping is expected to be complete by May 31, 2025.

The C-5 fleet is planned to retire in the 2040-time frame and will be recapitalised by the winner of the nascent C-X programme.

Rating the Super Galaxy

Given the accumulated years of operating F138 engine-powered C-5Ms, when asked how the 9th Airlift Squadron rates the General Electric F138 engines in terms of performance and reliability, Lieutenant Colonel Andrew Stein, 9th Airlift Squadron director of operations said: "The new engines are extremely capable. They allow the C-5M to take off with greater payloads, climbing to altitude more quickly, which results in a more fuel-efficient flight. The engines are also very reliable. Our maintenance counterparts will have specific data, but anecdotally, they have had very few issues."

Lockheed Martin originally sold the C-5M as an upgraded aircraft with shorter take-off, higher climb rate to initial altitude, increased cargo load, and longer-range performance. Lt Col Stein confirmed that all the performance aspects are accurate. He said: "The new M-model allows us to depart locations at max operating weights and fly direct to destinations we would not have been able to reach in previous models without a fuel stop or aerial refuelling. This capability saves time and money and allows for greater flexibility in mission planning as well as increased cargo throughput at our aerial ports. This also allows us to operate at challenging fields [short runways] in challenging environmental conditions [high temperatures and pressure altitudes] with greater cargo payloads than previously possible."

Ramp services technicians unload cargo from a transient aircraft at Dover Air Force Base. (US Air Force/Senior Airman Christopher Quail)

A ramp services technician listens to walkie-talkie communications while unloading cargo at Dover Air Force Base. (US Air Force/Senior Airman Christopher Quail)

vehicle is conducted on arrival at Dover. The vehicle then moves the fallen to the Port Mortuary at the Charles Carson Center for Mortuary Affairs. Once positively identified, fallen service members are prepared for transport to the destination determined by the family.

The Joint Personal Effects Depot (JPED) provides care and support to families and loved ones attending dignified transfers and processes the personal effects of service members from all service branches, as well as DoD civilians and contractors killed within theatre operations. The only organisation of its kind in the DoD, the JPED pioneered and advanced the care and handling of personal effects to ensure they are delivered to the person eligible to receive them in a presentable and timely manner.

Channel Missions

Air Mobility Command's most numerous and routine type of mission is the channel mission. These are regularly flown from Dover by C-5M and C-17A aircraft. The process for launching a channel mission starts with a set of validated

mission requirements submitted to the 618th Air Operations Centre (AOC) by US Transportation Command. Both organisations are based at Scott Air Force Base, Illinois.

For the purposes of this feature, we'll use two examples of channels flown from Dover. A C-17A loaded with palletised cargo bound for RAF Mildenhall, England and a C-5M carrying AH-64 Apache helicopters to Ramstein Air Base, Germany.

A component unit known as the 436th Current Operations receives the tasking from the AOC, then assigns each mission to a flying squadron, which assigns a crew, based on availability. All pertinent information is then relayed to the 436th Aircraft Maintenance Squadron, which assigns an aircraft to the mission.

Various sections in the 436th Aerial Port Squadron are involved. Each one has a direct impact on the missions to Mildenhall and Ramstein. For example, the fleet services section services every aircraft lavatory and delivers meals and expendables (such as earplugs, cups, water coolers and airsickness bags) to the assigned aircraft. Cargo is processed by the air terminal operations centre and managed by the air freight section.

When transporting AH-64 Apache attack helicopters to Ramstein loaded on a C-5M, the load planning is extremely important. Just consider putting hundreds of thousands of pounds of cargo onto a delicately balanced aircraft. Even the monstrous C-5M requires precision weight and balance to keep the aircraft aloft. Though the load plan is checked by several people before final approval, the aircraft loadmaster has final authority over the

Ramp services technicians unload cargo from a transient aircraft at Dover. Transient aircraft teams support over 1,300 aircraft per year. (US Air Force/Senior Airman Christopher Quail)

loading. In this case, the loadmaster would work with the US Army load team at the aircraft to ensure requirements are met. The last step of a multi-layered process to ensure, in this case the AH-64s get to their destination at the right time, in the right sequence.

In the case of the C-17 mission, the 618th AOC coordinates with the 436th Airlift Wing, whose C-17 loadmasters ensure the palletised cargo meets exacting specifications prior to loading.

Once that's all set-up, the aircrew is given a briefing about their forthcoming mission several days or weeks prior to departure.

C-5s and C-17s can be tasked dynamically (sometimes while in flight) to take on a last-minute, higher-priority mission. For this reason, aircrews are provided with the latest tools to make them worldwide capable at a moment's notice.

The ramp services section loads all aircraft at Dover Air Force Base, in concert with loadmasters and joint and total force partners – including other military branches, the Air Force Reserve, and the Air National Guard. Once en route, the mission loadmasters are responsible for loading and unloading cargo, with assistance from a local load team, such as one provided by the US Army.

Having flown to Mildenhall and Germany respectively, aircrews are authorised at least 17 hours of crew rest for food and sleep.

According to the 436th AW it is standard practice for the crew to stay with the same aircraft they departed with until they return to home-station.

A ramp services technician unloads cargo from a transient aircraft at Dover Air Force Base. (US Air Force/Senior Airman Christopher Quail)

Airmen palletise equipment bound for Ukraine during a foreign military sales mission at Dover Air Force Base on March 8, 2022. (US Air Force/TSgt Strong II)

An air transportation journeyman assigned to the 436th Aircraft Aerial Port Squadron, checks cargo on a C-5M Super Galaxy prior to the aircraft's departure for a direct delivery airlift mission. (US Air Force)

Aerial Port Squadron

Dubbed the Super Port, the 436th Aerial Port Squadron's primary mission is to provide airlift support for the movement of cargo, mail, and passengers to support the operations directed by the President of the United States, the Department of Defense, or the Joint Chiefs of Staff. In addition, the 436th Aerial Port Squadron provides airlift support of worldwide humanitarian efforts, exercises, contingencies, and emergencies.

The 436th APS provides different functions: processing personnel and cargo, rigging for airdrop, packing parachutes, loading equipment, preparing air cargo and load plans, loading, and securing aircraft, ejecting cargo for inflight delivery, and supervising units engaged in aircraft loading and unloading operations.

These functions are undertaken by personnel assigned to six sections.

- Air terminal operations centre functions as a command element in charge of information control and dissemination.
- Load planning section configures all the aircraft loads.
- Special handling section inspects and processes hazardous materials transiting aircraft.
- Ramp section comprises the material handling equipment operators that load the aircraft.
- Passenger section runs the passenger terminal, processing passengers for air travel.
- Cargo section conducts pallet build-up and cargo manifesting.

The 436th Aerial Port Squadron runs a passenger terminal at Dover. The primary mission of the terminal is to provide efficient and expeditious airlift support for the movement of cargo, mail, personal

C-17A Globemaster III

Reckoned to be the most flexible cargo aircraft to enter the airlift force, the C-17 is capable of rapid delivery of troops and all types of cargo to main operating bases or directly to forward bases in a deployment area. The aircraft conducts inter- and intra-theatre missions, tactical airlift and airdrop missions and can transport litters of ambulatory patients during aeromedical evacuations.

Inter-theatre operations are between two or more geographic combatant commands and intra-theatre operations are exclusively within one geographic combatant command.

Boeing, which acquired McDonnell Douglas in 1997, delivered the last of 222 Globemaster IIIs to the US Air Force in September 2013.

Powered by four Pratt & Whitney F117-PW-100 turbofan engines, the C-17A can carry up to 102 troops, 36 litter patients, or 18 standard 463L cargo pallets.

Since entering service, the fleet has received numerous upgrades that included integration of a Large Infrared Countermeasures (LAIRCM) system and a new weather radar.

The US Air Force Life Cycle Management Center's C-17 Program Office completed Block 21 upgrades on the entire world fleet of 275 C-17 aircraft operated by the US Air Force and eight allied countries.

Block 21 included the installation of hardware and software associated with the Automatic Dependent Surveillance-Broadcast Out (ADS-B Out) transponder system mentioned in the C-5M section. As a reminder, the system broadcasts the precise position and location information of an aircraft in real time, giving air traffic control improved visibility and providing aircrew with more situational awareness of nearby aircraft.

Block 21 also included identification friend or foe (IFF) transponder Mode 5 modifications and communication/navigation capability and software updates to improve the aircraft's flight management systems.

Improvements to the C-17's beyond line-of sight communication systems and a replacement head-up display are also being installed.

A C-17A Globemaster III completes a touch and go landing at Dover Air Force Base. (US Air Force/Roland Balik)

Airmen from the 436th Aerial Port Squadron load cargo onto a Kalitta Air Boeing 747.
(US Air Force/Senior Airman Zachary Cacicia)

property, and passengers in support of contingency, and peacetime operations. Domestic destinations served are Charleston Air Force Base, South Carolina, Joint Base Lewis-McChord, Washington, and Travis Air Force, California. International destinations are Ramstein Air Base, Germany, Spangdahlem Air Base, Germany, and Naval Air Station Rota, Spain.

Just like passengers using commercial airlines, 'space-available' passengers must comply with baggage allowance requirements and abide by all Transportation Security Administration guidelines and requirements.

At Dover, an enormous aerial port facility is a vital building used by the 436th APS to process cargo in the air bridge that sustains American forces assigned to EUCOM, AFRICOM and CENTCOM.

In March 2020, 22,000 tons of aircraft cargo was processed through the aerial port on inbound and outbound missions: the highest monthly total since Desert Storm in March 1991.

At the peak of the March 2020 operation, the 426th APS was building around 150 aircraft pallets per day and loaded or unloaded more than 150 commercial 747

aircraft and completed more than 500 up- and downloads on C-5 and C-17 aircraft.

The Traffic Management Office managed more than 1,900 inbound and outbound cargo trucks during March 2020.

As an example, at the time 80 members of the 436th APS deployed to locations in the US Central Command's area of operations to receive and process inbound and outbound cargo.

At the time, the 436th APS managed more than 200 passengers transiting through the passenger terminal each week. Its fleet services branch also clean and prepare each departing aircraft for the crew and passengers.

During the early months of the COVID-19 pandemic, 436th APS capability forecasters working in collaboration with the 618th AOC Channel Requirement Branch devised a new and more efficient way to plan and execute mobility missions on both military and commercial aircraft. Capability forecasters are tasked with maximising aircraft utilisation and ensuring that logistics run smoothly.

Missions were rerouted via Dover; the cargo then entered the local port and was permitted to share space utilisation

on scheduled airlifts rather than on commercial flights that cost a significant amount of money. Additionally, the amount of time cargo spent on the ground was reduced to two or three hours.

Saving Money

According to the 436th AW's public affairs office the 436th Aerial Port Squadron saved approximately $5m through collaborative efforts with the 618th AOC to reroute and resource cargo missions through the installation despite complications caused by the pandemic.

Bradley Schmidt, 436th APS cargo scheduler said: "In some instances, [before COVID] an aircraft used to come in and spend 24-48 hours [on the flight line] before it took off to go back home. They're now spending two or three hours here: just enough time for us to get cargo off, new cargo on, and then they go to their next location."

The combination of COVID-19 procedures and limited time for ground operations required the APS to collaborate and devise a new and more efficient way to plan and execute mobility missions on a combination of both military and commercial aircraft.

Capability forecasters tasked with maximising aircraft utilisation and ensuring that logistics run smoothly work with the 618th AOC's channel requirement branch, to coordinate conflict-free cargo missions.

Destiny Donigan, 436th APS cargo scheduling supervisor and capability forecaster, recognised how many empty C-5Ms and C-17As were leaving Dover towards cargo destinations. Through coordination with the 618th AOC's channel requirement branch, Donigan and her team managed to get missions re-routed via Dover. This permitted cargo to be moved on Dover-based C-5s and C-17s rather than using commercial flights that cost a significant amount of money. The cargo was then allowed to enter the local port and permitted shared space utilisation on scheduled airlifts.

K-Loaders carrying cargo pallets preposition prior to an upload of a Kalitta Air Boeing 747 at Dover. Kalitta Air is a member of the Civil Reserve Air Fleet, a mobility resource contractually committed to support Department of Defense airlift requirements in emergencies and when the need for airlift exceeds military aircraft capability. (US Air Force/Senior Airman Zachary Cacicia)

Re-routing gets the cargo to destinations on time, if not ahead of schedule.

Brigadier General Daniel DeVoe, 618th Air Operations Center commander said: "Through our strategic partnership with the 436th APS and our recent transformation, the 618th AOC applied innovative solutions, delivered cargo faster and saved the taxpayer nearly $5 million."

Aerial Port of the Future

As part of the US Air Force's Aerial Port of the Future initiative a new system known as the Configured Air Load Building Tool or CALBT is being developed to modernise Air Mobility Command's cargo handling processes.

The CALBT system consists of light detection and ranging cameras which enable 3D images of cargo received to be created, and hand-held tablets loaded with software that enable efficient pallet building.

Increased pallet space utilisation from an estimated 75% to 80 to 90% and optimisation of cargo flow are the main objectives of the CALBT.

The CALBT system should fit into the Aerial Port of the Future by efficiently automating the process of how an aerial port accepts cargo and pushes that cargo through the port's facilities and onto the aircraft, and how cargo is received into the port.

The 436th APS evaluated the CALBT at Dover.

Operations and Management Information System

Air Mobility Command's aerial port operations and management information system was adopted in the 1990s. Dubbed GATES, the Global Air Transportation Execution System was designed to support automated cargo and passenger processing, the reporting of in-transit visibility data to the Global Transportation Network, and billing to Air Mobility Command's financial management directorate. The system remains in use with Air Mobility Command's Aerial Port Squadrons.

The Cargo Movement Operational System, dubbed CMOS is another legacy system used by the traffic management office assigned to each APS. Its function is to streamline contingency and sustainment cargo and passenger movement processes.

According to the 436th APS: "CMOS imports shipment requirements for

Airmen from the 436th Aerial Port Squadron load cargo onto a Kalitta Air Boeing 747. (US Air Force/Senior Airman Zachary Cacicia)

Cargo pallets are loaded into a Kalitta Air Boeing 747 cargo plane by airmen assigned to the 436th Aerial Port Squadron at Dover. Unlike military airlifters that load cargo from a rear or forward ramp, a Boeing 747 loads cargo through a side door. (US Air Force/Senior Airman Zachary Cacicia)

military standard requisitioning and issue procedures, personnel, and deployment planning systems. It supports shipment planning through interfaces with various military cargo management systems and commercial carrier systems. CMOS also undertakes load planning via an interface with the integrated computerised deployment system, dubbed ICODES. CMOS produces labels, radio frequency identification tags, hazardous material, and commercial/military movement documentation, and provides in-transit visibility (ITV) data to down line stations.

Both GATES and CMOS are used by the 436th APS for the sustainment and strategic airlift missions. However, sometimes they do not interface with one another.

The Air Force Research Laboratory evaluated CALBT as part of a small business innovative research project with the objective to develop autonomous software and hardware tools for automating the load building process and receiving process into an aerial port.

CALBT testing conducted by the 436th APS used actual cargo delivered by trucks and unloaded at the docks.

According to the 436th APS: "Without the CALBT, airmen handle and process a piece of cargo between seven and ten times, from the moment it is received until it is put on a pallet.

By incorporating CALBT, Air Mobility Command hopes to reduce the number of times cargo is handled by 50%. This is achieved by using genetic algorithms to consider different goals and objectives and different constraints to determine an optimal solution for streamlining the pallet building process.

The 436th APS says the CALBT initiative seeks to automate and optimise the pallet building process by taking 3D scans of incoming packages, establish their dimensions and determine the information listed on the shipping label. Air transportation specialists, colloquially known as Port Dawgs use a tablet loaded with the CALBT software to scan shipping labels. Information such as the transportation control number, priority, hazards, and weight become readily available.

Airmen from the 436th Aerial Port Squadron load cargo onto a Kalitta Air Boeing 747. (US Air Force/Senior Airman Zachary Cacicia)

Airmen from the 436th Aerial Port Squadron load cargo onto a Kalitta Air Boeing 747. (US Air Force/Senior Airman Zachary Cacicia)

Airmen from the 436th Aerial Port Squadron load cargo onto a Kalitta Air Boeing 747. (US Air Force/Senior Airman Zachary Cacicia)

Recent Ops

Amidst a 300% mission surge in September 2022, the 436th APS used multi-capable airmen from the 436th Maintenance Squadron to assist with building cargo onto aircraft pallets. Utilisation of maintainers enabled the 436th APS to sustain the airlift requirements in support of Ukraine, while continuing to support ongoing channel missions to US European Command, US Africa Command and US Central Command.

Within 48 hours of the devastating earthquakes in Turkey on February 5, 2023, 436th APS airmen processed US humanitarian assistance in support of search and rescue efforts. The 436th APS processed and loaded 83 passengers and 58,000lb of cargo from the US Agency for International Development onto an Alaska Air National Guard C-17.

Among the passengers were urban search and rescue personnel and six dogs from Fairfax County, Virginia. The team comprised structural engineers, doctors, logistics personnel and technical search specialists. Cargo included concrete breakers and generators, medical supplies, tents, water, and water purification systems.

As one of two search and rescue teams that respond on behalf of the US government, the team was in Turkey less than 24 hours from initial notification with enough supplies to sustain operations for at least seven days.

In 2003 a storage warehouse used by the 436th APS suffered a roof collapse

C-5M Super Galaxy 87-0035 taxis from the gargantuan flight line at Dover Air Force Base. (US Air Force/Greg Davis)

A US Army CH-47D Chinook helicopter emerges from a C-5M Super Galaxy during unloading at Dover Air Force Base. (US Air Force/Greg Davis)

With a cargo compartment 13ft 6in high by 19ft wide by 143ft 9in long, the C5M can accommodate pretty much anything the USAF needs to move. (US Air Force/Greg Davis)

A head-on shot of a US Army CH-47D Chinook helicopter being unloaded from a C-5M Super Galaxy at Dover Air Force Base. (US Air Force/Greg Davis)

which affected output capability of the aerial port. Consequently, some channel missions were transferred to the 305th APS based at Joint Base McGuire-Dix-Lakehurst, New Jersey.

Last year AMC and TRANSCOM made a joint decision to move the channel missions bound for Europe from McGuire back to Dover. The decision was based on the channel support required by US European Command and dwindling support required for US Central Command theatres. Re-acquiring the channel missions added approximately 24 missions for the 436th APS to oversee each month. The combined demand of both commands represents a large part of the airlift delivered from Dover.

C-130J Hercules

Air Mobility Command's 317th Airlift Wing based at Dyess Air Force Base is the largest C-130J unit in the world.

The first C-130J Super Hercules was delivered to the base on February 9, 2012. At the end of its transition from the C-130H model to the C-130J Super Hercules, the 317th AW had 28 aircraft assigned.

The fleet is shared by the 39th and 40th Airlift Squadrons tasked with airlift and aeromedical missions. Many of the individual missions flown from Dyess stage through one of Air Mobility Command's aerial ports such as Charleston Air Force Base, South Carolina, Joint Base McGuire-Dix-Lakehurst, New Jersey, and Travis Air Force Base, California to pick-up cargo.

The aircrew usually make a night stop at the aerial port and fly to the cargo's destination the following day.

At the aerial port, a standard air land cargo loadout is delivered to the aircraft by a ramp crew assigned to air freight section. The crew includes spotters to watch the loading process from the K loader and on to the aircraft.

Before any cargo is loaded, the loadmaster inspects all cargo to ensure it is serviceable, will fit the aircraft's hold, verifies the weights, ensures it is air worthy for flight, and meets all aircraft limitations.

The C-130J is equipped with systems that help the loadmaster to load and unload. These include flip-up rollers that

pop out of the floor when a pin is pulled, computer-controlled locks for locking and unlocking the cargo to the floor, a multifunctional control display which calculates the aircraft's centre-of-gravity when the loadmaster enters the flight limits, the cargo weight, and its location.

The loadmaster holds overall responsibility for the loading process collaborating with the spotters and can stop the process and re-direct, as necessary. Once checked, the cargo is loaded and locked to the floor. Then the loadmaster ensures the centre-of-gravity limits match the computer system's calculations. Once the centre-of-gravity is verified, the air land load is ready for its flight to the destination.

The Big Three Hundred

Legacies do not come much bigger than the A300, it was the company's first jet and the bedrock for every type that followed. The freighter version remains in service with multiple operators, not least DHL, FedEx, and UPS.

Of the many objectives for the A300, Airbus aimed to provide an intermediate twin-engine aircraft to compete against the Boeing 727, Douglas DC-10, and Lockheed L-1011 trijets, with capacity to hold side-by-side LD3 cargo containers in the lower hold.

Innovations used included triple hydraulic and electric systems, an advanced aft-loaded wing section, automatic throttles controlling thrust at all speeds, wind-shear detection to ensure availability of full power and equipment permitting crews to fly at maximum-lift angle of attack. A tall undercarriage ensured ground clearance

beneath the large underwing pylon-mounted fan engines.

Other developments included Krueger flaps for hot-and-high operations, a

An A300-600F in the colours of FedEx Express at Toulouse-Blagnac in 2007. (Airbus/H Gousse)

side cargo door for convertible freight operations and, more significantly, the forward-facing crew concept that gave the world the two-pilot airliner cockpit.

Both the A300 and the A310 gained a new lease of life as freighters, primarily through the conversion of existing airliners in the case of the A310, and as new build aircraft and conversions in the case of the A300.

The A300 makes for a good freighter given its 222in fuselage cross section, a main deck cargo loading system which enables 96in pallets to be carried side-by-side, the ability to carry standard LD3 containers and cargo pallets in the lower cargo hold, and a new floor structure to accommodate heavy loads.

The longer-range A300-600R passenger plane developed for American Airlines preceded the A300-600RF freighter. Airbus received an order for 25 aircraft from Federal Express (FedEx) in 1991, the first of which flew in December 1993. FedEx received its first A300-600RF in 1994 and subsequently ordered another 17 jets. The integrator went on to buy

A300-600F JA02GX (msn 872) was delivered to Japanese cargo carrier Galaxy Airlines in April 2006. (Airbus)

other second hand 600Fs such that its current fleet totals 65.

Demand for the A300 slowed during the second half of the 1990s, as the commercial aviation marketplace changed, and more modern types offered greater efficiency. The last passenger version was handed over to Japan Air System in November 2002, but freighters continued to be produced. The 561st and final production A300, an A300F freighter for FedEx made its first flight on April 18, 2007.

Cargo Operations

US-based cargo airline FedEx Express is the world's biggest A300 operator, with 65 aircraft in use. The Federal Express Corporation is based in Memphis, Tennessee, and delivers freight and packages to more than 375 destinations in more than 220 countries across six continents each day.

UPS Airlines is a wholly owned subsidiary of UPS (United Parcel Service) and is the second-largest cargo airline worldwide (in terms of freight volume flown) and is today also the world's second biggest operator of the A300, with 52 aircraft. Ironically, the A300 is a small player in the UPS fleet, which also includes 75 Boeing 757-200Fs and 80 767-300s, with more on order. The UPS fleet of 52 A300s have a long future though and are currently undergoing a flight deck upgrade based around Honeywell Primus

Epic avionics; new displays and flight management system (FMS), improved weather radar, a central maintenance system, and a new version of the current enhanced ground proximity warning system. This is intended to allow them to serve until 2035, and with a relatively light utilisation rate of only two to three cycles per day, they will not have reached their maximum number of cycles by then.

A group of cargo airlines that are owned, co-owned or chartered by DHL Express operate their A300s in DHL's distinctive livery. Some 22 of these are operated by European Air Transport Leipzig, four by Ireland's ASL Airlines and there is one aircraft with Slovenia's Solinair. European Air Transport Leipzig GmbH is a German cargo airline wholly owned by Deutsche Post and that operates the group's DHL-branded parcel and express services and provides ad hoc charter services including livestock transport. ASL was originally established as Air Bridge Carriers at East Midlands Airport, subsequently becoming Hunting Cargo Airlines and eventually Air Contractors.

Air Hong Kong's nine A300s wear a hybrid DHL livery, with a white forward fuselage but with a yellow tailfin and rear fuselage, and yellow engine nacelles.

A wholly owned subsidiary of Cathay Pacific Airlines, Air Hong Kong is focused on providing air cargo services to DHL Express, operating a regular DHL Express schedule between Hong Kong and Bangkok, Beijing, Cebu, Chengdu, Ho Chi Minh City, Manila, Nagoya, Osaka,

Airbus A300F4-600R Freighter Characteristics	
Length	177ft 5in (54.08m)
Cabin length	133ft 6in (40.69m)
Fuselage width	18ft 6in (5.64m)
Max cabin width	17ft 4in (5.28m)
Wingspan	147ft 1in (44.83m)
Wing area	2,798ft^2 (2,582m^2)
Wing sweep	28°
Tail height	54ft 8in (16.66m)
Fuselage height	25ft (7.62m)
Track	31ft 6in (9.6m)
Wheelbase	61ft (18.59m)
Ceiling	40,000ft (12,192m)
Range	4,050nm (7,500km)
Cruise speed	450kts (833kph)
Mmo	Mach 0.82
Max ramp weight	377,870lb (171,3998kg)
Max take-off weight	375,890lb (170,500kg)
Max landing weight	308,650lb (140,000kg)
Max zero fuel weight	286,600lb (130,000kg)
Max fuel capacity	18,000 US gal (68,137lit)
Primary cargo door at the forward fuselage	141 x 101in (3.58 x 2.56m)
Cargo volume main deck	19,070ft^3 (540m^3)
Cargo volume lower deck	5,580ft^3 (158m^3)
Unit load devices main deck	43 AYYs 15 pallets in single-row loading sized 96 x 96 x 125in or 21 pallets in side-by-side loading sized 88 x 96 x 125in
Unit load devices lower deck	22 LD3s
Engines	Two GE CF6-80C2s or two P&W 4158s
Maiden flight	July 8, 1983

(AirTeamImages/Jan Ostrowski)

Wearing the UPS United Parcel Services livery, A300-600F msn 848 (F-WWAZ) takes off at Toulouse-Blagnac in June 2004. (Airbus/H Gousse)

Penang, Seoul, Singapore, Shanghai, Taipei, and Tokyo. Cathay's A300s are now being replaced by Airbus A330-200 and A330-300 Freighters.

In Turkey, MNG Airlines is a cargo airline headquartered in Istanbul, operating four A300s, with another example currently parked. In 2005, MNG won an award from Airbus for 100% reliability on the 30-year-old Airbus A300. On February 6, 2006, MNG ceased all passenger flights, but continued with cargo flights.

Airbus itself operates four A300-600ST (Super Transporter), or Beluga cargo aircraft, with a fifth presently out of use. Demand for these Airbus Beluga Transports increased markedly and saw additional demand after sanctions were imposed on Russia following its invasion of Ukraine in February 2022 effectively halting services by Russian- and Ukrainian-operated Antonov An-124s.

Elsewhere, Mexico's AeroUnion (Aerotransporte de Carga Unión S.A. de C.V.), operates cargo services within Mexico and between Mexico and the United States with a fleet that includes two Airbus A300-600Fs, one Airbus A300C4-600 and two Boeing 767-200Fs.

AeroUnion operates scheduled cargo services from its HQ in Hangar Zone G at Mexico City International Airport. Another Latin American A300 operator, Caracas-based Transcarga International Airways C.A. operates domestic charter cargo services with a pair of Airbus A300B4Fs. In 2020, Transcarga founded a Panamanian subsidiary, Cargo Three which is due to operate an Airbus A300B4F on non-scheduled services operating between the US and Panama. A former AeroUnion A300B4-203F (XA-FPP) is flying in a basic Transcarga colour scheme with Cargo Three titles.

There are several operators who have only a single A300 freighter, including Aerostan, Kap.kg and Moalem Aviation in Kyrgyzstan, Afriqiyah Airways in Libya, and Easy Charter in Georgia, where AMS Airlines still has one or two stored A300s.

The A310 freighter is an even rarer bird. FedEx Express ended A310-300(F) operations on January 4, 2020, with a flight from Sioux Falls to Memphis. The company ferried its remaining aircraft to Victorville for scrapping. In Turkey, ULS Airlines Cargo retains three A310s, while Royal Jordanian has a single example in service. Only one of the A310s used by Tajikistan's Asia Sky Lines remains in the company's hands, and it has been parked since September 2022.

Wearing its Airbus test registration F-WWAZ, A300-600F (msn 848) seen at Toulouse-Blagnac in June 2004. (Airbus/H Gousse)

Workhorse Twin

The popularity of the legacy Airbus A330 is reflected by a large operator base and continued investments to keep them fresh.

January 2023 marked 29 years since the Airbus A330 entered service, both the A330-200 and the A330-300 have been very successful products for the framer. Despite the longevity of the A330-200 and A330-300 (now referred to as A330ceos) and the A330-900neo and A330-800neo variants

launched in 2014 and offering double-digit savings in fuel burn, emissions and operational costs on their forebears, the appeal of the A330ceo models endures.

The first A330s in the tripartite co-operative venture between Airbus, ST Aerospace and EFW covering passenger-to-freighter conversions for A330-200s

and A330-300s delivered its first A330-300 P2F aircraft to DHL Express in 2017.

With a requirement for over 2,400 dedicated mid-sized freighters over the next 20 years they remain at the core of the market. The A330-200F can serve efficiently big airports such as Hong Kong, Shanghai, and Frankfurt, while allowing

The first section of A330-200F F-WWYE (c/n MSN1004) in Airbus colours on the assembly line at Toulouse-Blagnac. (Airbus/Christian Brinkmann)

Ground handlers position a K-loader alongside the A330-200F on the stand at the Airbus customer delivery centre at Toulouse. (Key-Mark Ayton)

profitable operations on secondary but high yield routes where the capacity of larger freighters does not make sense.

The airlines that operate the A330-200F midsize freighters are properly geared to match capacity with demand on all markets without relying solely on trunk routes. The A330-200F is marketed as an ideal replacement for old generation freighters, Airbus says it also provides airlines with an efficient solution to complement larger freighters and belly cargo.

According to Airbus: "The A330-200F has payload, range, and economics superior to previous generation freighters, carrying 70 tonnes with a range up to 4,000nm (7,400km) and provides similar unit costs compared to larger freighters. Its versatile main deck accommodates standard industry pallets and containers, but also enables carriage of oversized cargo with 16ft and 20ft pallets."

Derived from the A330 jetliner family, the A330-200F is a purpose-built freighter that adapts the proven technologies of the passenger variant to the needs of cargo operations. It features a common flight deck with the A330 passenger variant and virtually identical flying qualities with the A320, A340, A350XWB and A380 Families. Consequently, a pilot already qualified on the passenger variant only requires computer-based training to transition to the all-cargo version.

In day-to-day operations the A330 freighter flies between 350 and 400 hours per month, which is equivalent to large freighter aircraft.

According to Airbus: "Larger freighters struggle to gather sufficient payload to reach profitability, resulting in more risk and lower frequencies. So, the A330-200F was launched to answer the need for efficient, midsize aircraft that could be operated on thinner, or frequency driven markets with economics equivalent to those of larger freighters. For example, at 70 tonnes, the A330-200F cost per tonne is 35% lower than that of a larger freighter. Fuel-efficient technologies, flexible cargo configurations and optimised load factors help to make the A330-200F a cost-efficient freighter."

Generally, freight flies only one way, creating flow imbalances with differences in loads and yields for out-bound and in-bound services. Airbus highlights how imbalances can have a dramatic impact if low loads are combined with low yields: "Hence, the larger the aircraft the deeper is the loss on the weak leg."

The then new A330-200F offered greater range and a higher maximum payload with much lower unit costs compared with its closest competitor, the Boeing 777F.

According to Airbus: "Compared to an older DC-10 with a similar payload, an A330-200F operator can save 70% costs, thanks to more efficient fuel burn, engines, and much lower maintenance costs. Compared to a Boeing 747-400, the 200F yields approximately the same unit costs, same cost per ton on the 200F as the 747-400F, albeit a smaller payload."

Depending on the planned mission, the A330-200F can carry more than 141,000lb (64 tonnes) over 4,000nm (7,400km), or more than 152,000lb (69 tonnes) up to 3,200nm (5,930km) - non-stop. The range and payload capabilities enable operators to open new cargo routes or extend those already in operation.

Configured with an optimised fuselage cross-section enables the A330-200F to carry a variety of pallet and container sizes for maximum interlining capability, offering 30% more volume than any freighter in the 30 to 80 tonne midsize class.

A330F First Flight

The new dedicated freighter variant of the successful A330 Family made its maiden flight from Toulouse on November 4, 2009. Powered by Pratt & Whitney PW4000 engines, A330-200F F-WWYE (msn 1004) completed the 3-hour 50-minute flight with Airbus test pilots Philippe Perrin and Martin Scheuermann at the controls, accompanied by flight test engineers Wolfgang Brueggemann, Stephane Vaux, and Pascal Verneau. The maiden flight kicked-off a 180-hour flight-test and certification campaign. European Aviation Safety Agency and Federal Aviation Administration certification was awarded in April 2010.

"The airframe is behaving wonderfully," exclaimed Perrin after flying the A330-200F for the first time.

"We have 200 more hours of flight-testing to complete over the next three months to open up the flight envelope."

The former astronaut spoke of the need to "allow the aircraft to fly to a maximum CG of 15"," to improve the flexibility when loading pallets of various weights throughout the main deck. This is 3% higher than the passenger version.

As part of the flight-testing performed on the maiden flight the crew tested the landing gear. It is attached at a lower level than the passenger version to adjust the nose-attitude and housed in an external fairing with new doors. According to Perrin the doors "functioned very well, we extended the gear in normal and abnormal configurations, at different speeds, and the fairing caused no noise or buffeting."

In terms of the flight domain, Perrin said: "We flew at 330kts (610km/h) which

A330-200F Facts

- A330-200F programme launched in January 2007.
- First firm orders placed in summer of 2007.
- A reinforced fuselage to improve shear and bending for more loading flexibility and higher weight.
- A strengthened floor with a specially designed floor-grid for higher running loads.
- An increase in maximum-zero-fuel weight by 17,600lb (eight tonnes) which enables the aircraft to carry 70 tonnes of cargo in a 10lb/ft³ high-density configuration.
- A cargo loading system that caters for all standard unit loading devices (ULDs), pallets or containers.
- A 101 x 141in door to enable use of all types of ULD
- Lower attachment points of the standard A330 nose landing gear in a modified landing gear bay, fairing

- and doors to minimise the aircraft's nose-down attitude to ease loading.
- A 9g barrier wall between the customisable courier area and the main hold with two access doors. The barrier is designed to prevent loose cargo from impacting the courier area.
- The first metal was cut for aircraft msn 1004 in March 2008; the first fuselage mated in January 2009; final assembly of aircraft msn 1004 started on June 28, 2009.
- A330-200F F-WWYE (msn 1004) took off from Toulouse-Blagnac on its maiden flight at 10:05AM on November 4, 2009.
- Post-flight test, the aircraft re-entered the Toulouse production line to have its test equipment removed and to be readied for delivery.
- Airbus delivered 38 A330-200F aircraft, the last of them in February 2017.

is above the maximum permissible speed of the A330 pax version, and to a very low Alpha Max speed, exploring the flight domain to extremes, except that today we stayed within the normal A330 payload CG envelope, flying beyond that envelope takes more time and technique."

One component of the flight-test programme involved opening the flight envelope to gain extreme centre of gravity (CG) of 15° with the objective of extending the aircraft's CG by 3%. This test programme was designed to improve the aircraft's flexibility for loading freight pallets of varying weights throughout the aircraft's main deck cargo bay.

The crew also tested the modified nose-gear arrangement, which incorporates an external blimp fairing to accommodate the lower leg attachment needed to ensure the aircraft sits level on the ground for

Airbus personnel opened up the 101 x 141-inch (2.56 x 3.58m) cargo door to show the utility of the A330-200F for loading all UDLs. (Key-Mark Ayton)

Capt Philip Perrin performed a touch and go as part of the November 4, 2009 demo of the A330-200F. This shot shows the nose landing gear fairing and new doors.

Airbus was rightly confident in its A330-200F at launch. The aircraft was adorned with the statement 'the right aircraft, right time'. (Key-Mark Ayton)

loading. Perrin said: "We wanted to check the operation of the new doors, which worked well, nor were there any noise or buffet issues with the fairing. We flew two auto-land approaches at Toulouse, including a late go-around and a touch-and-go, before making a full-stop landing."

Phillip Perrin confirmed that the aircraft was to undergo hot and cold weather testing and expected the flight test programme to be complete by March 2010 when the company hoped to gain simultaneous certification by the European Aviation Safety Agency and US Federal Aviation Administration.

As the aircraft pulled on to the stand at the customer delivery centre nobody could be in any doubt of the confidence Airbus had in its latest model. Emblazoned along the port side fuselage was the statement 'the right aircraft, right now', quite a statement considering the market slump at the time, and one that Tom Williams, the then executive vice president of programmes was challenged on during the press conference. "When we develop a programme, we develop it for 20, 30 years, we don't worry about the window of five or six months. If you look at our 20-year global market forecast, we are forecasting 5.2% average annual growth in terms of ton-kilometres," replied the Scotsman. At the time Airbus forecast a market requirement of 3,400 freighters over the next 20 years including 1,600 mid-sized like the A330-200F.

At the time of the first flight, the then Airbus chief operating officer John Leahy went further. "We are at the eve of a market recovery, and now is the time for

airlines to prepare for future freight growth," he said.

Prior to the maiden flight Airbus had already completed testing using a 200-series pax aircraft. Fuel control and computer monitoring validation was completed during ground tests. During a ten-flight programme Airbus evaluated the aircraft's handling qualities with a modified CG and increased maximum landing weight to simulate freighter ops. Some initial autopilot tests were also undertaken. One test involved temperature measurement on the lower deck with the main cargo deck at 5°C to determine performance of electrical and hydraulic systems.

A second phase with the A330-200F covered performance and calibration, further handling qualities, stall, buffet, and landing gear testing. It also tested flight management, navigation, communication, autopilot, smoke detection and air conditioning systems.

Commenting on the A330-200F flight test programme, Tom Williams, then Airbus commercial aircraft executive VP programmes said: "When flying cargo, you want to know if the door is there and that the pressure holds. The pressure was holding very well. We had a very tight structure. We have new air-conditioning and electrical systems, more wiring - we must ensure everything is safe. We have to look at the landing gear because we extended the nose landing gear, with new doors, they functioned very well, we extended the gear in different configurations, normal and abnormal, at different speeds. And we flew above

the maximum allowed speed of the A330 passenger version, we went to a very low Alpha max speed, exploring the flight domain to extremes."

In-Service Fleet

Earlier-vintage A330-300 variants (pre-2000) likely with lower maximum take-off weight are operationally less-flexible

(Key-Mark Ayton)

and thus may be less attractive to new passenger operators but may represent an opportunity for the freighter [conversion] programme.

The first A330s in the tripartite co-operative venture between Airbus, ST Aerospace and EFW covering passenger-to-freighter conversions for A330-200s and A330-300s delivered its first aircraft to DHL Express in Q4 2017.

On January 17, 2007, Guggenheim Aviation Partners, a US-based aviation investment firm, became the first customer to sign a contract for the A330-200F. The aircraft were acquired for Flyington Freighters, a cargo airline company based at Hyderabad, India. According to the Air Cargo News website: "Flyington Freighters was founded in 2006 in Hyderabad and was to be the launch customer of Airbus' new A330-200 freighter in July 2008, having 12 on order. The freighter type suffered a string of delays and Flyington shut down while waiting."

Airbus also offered the A330-200F powered by Rolls-Royce Trent 700 engines, the powerplant chosen by Etihad Airways. Its first aircraft, registration A6-DCA (msn 1032) was delivered in August 2010.

A330-200 Freighter Configurations

- Range mode enables a 64 metric ton payload to be flown over 4,000nm (7,400km) yielded by the three-ton increase of the zero-fuel weight.
- Payload mode enables a 69-tonne payload to be flown up to 3,200nm (5,930km) non-stop yielded by the eight-tonne increase of the zero-fuel weight.
- Both modes are offered simultaneously, which means the operator can fly in one direction with range mode and with payload mode in the other direction depending on the loads to be carried.
- Lower unit costs compared to its closest competitor.
- Maximum interlining capability.
- 30% more volume than any freighter in its class.
- High-density cargo configuration of 10lb/ft^3.
- Engine options: Pratt & Whitney PW4000 or Rolls-Royce Trent 700.

Out of UKRAINE

Antonov's giant An-124 Ruslan was designed to carry heavy and outsize cargo. Alexander Mladenov reviews the type.

The An-124 was developed in the late 1970s by the Kyiv-based Antonov Design Bureau to meet a Soviet Air Force requirement for a super heavy transport aircraft with better performance than its US rival, the Lockheed C-5 Galaxy. Its design was launched following a Soviet Council of Ministers decree dated February 1972. Initially, Antonov proposed a rather conservative design, which was shelved in 1976. Instead, much more advanced technical solutions were conceived for the new machine, which was externally like the C-5 and borrowed some design specifics from it, such as the upward-hinging nose and kneeling landing gear to facilitate easier cargo hold access. The new four-engine military transport, dubbed Ruslan and known in NATO as *Condor*, featured a raft of cutting-edge technologies never used before on such a class of aircraft in the Soviet Union. The list of novelties included supercritical wing profile and a fly-by-wire flight control system to enhance performance,

Antonov Airlines' An-124-100M
Ruslan UR-82027 on take-off from
Warsaw-Chopin International Airport.
(AirTeamImages/Jan Ostrowski)

together with advanced production methods and materials for the large-size airframe structure components to save weight. In addition, the new aircraft got an all-new engine, the Ivchenko-Progress D-18T high-bypass ratio turbofan, the first of its kind to be designed and built in the Soviet Union.

The first Ruslan prototype, c/n 01-01, wearing the Soviet civil registration CCCP-680125, entered assembly at the Antonov experimental plant in Kyiv in 1979 and was rolled out on October 24, 1982, while the maiden flight followed suit on December 24, 1982; Antonov test pilot Vladimir Tersky was the captain on board. The initial period of testing was plagued by the disappointingly low reliability of the D-18T engine, which continued to be a serious issue even as the type entered service with the Soviet Air Force in 1987 and persisted in the following decade.

The second airframe built at Antonov, c/n 01-02, was used for static tests, while the first production-standard aircraft, 01-03, was produced at Kyiv, in the plant known as Aviant, with the first flight made in December 1984. Sadly, it was lost in a crash on October 13, 1987, due to a bird strike and a subsequent destruction of the nose radome with fragments ingested by three engines causing catastrophic damage.

The second plant in the Soviet Union engaged in the An-124's series-production was newly built in Ulyanovsk in Russia, now known as Aviastar-SP. Its first aircraft, c/n 01-07, took to the air for the first time in October 1985. A total of 96 Ruslans were originally planned to be built for the Soviet Air Force, 36 of these at the Kyiv plant and 60 more in Ulyanovsk, in addition to two Antonov-built airframes. In the event, the abrupt breakup of the Soviet Union shelved these plans and in the 1990s the An-124 production was sharply reduced; in the 2000s, only single aircraft were rolled out at both plants, delivered to civilian customers only.

The total production run accounted for 54 series produced Ruslans, including 18 in Kyiv and 36 more in Ulyanovsk. The final machine built at Aviant in Kyiv took to the air for the first time in October 2003, while the last Aviastar-SP-built Ruslan made its first flight in April 2004.

Currently, the biggest An-124 operator is the Russian Air and Space Force (RuASF), with a total fleet of 26 aircraft operated by the 566th VTAP (military air transport regiment) at Sescha in the west of the country. Of the 20 aircraft once in commercial service, Volga-Dnepr's fleet of 11 are all parked-up in storage, five remain in operation with Antonov Airlines of Ukraine, and one is owned by Maximus Air Cargo of the United Arab Emirates. The others are in storage.

Civilian Operation

It is noteworthy that the mass use of the An-124 in the commercial air transport world since 1991 has become possible thanks to the very low purchase price of the aircraft at the time. This enabled the aircraft to be used in a very profitable manner from the very beginning.

The civil Ruslan version, designated the An-124-100, was certificated in December 1992 by the Intestate Aviation Committee (a civil aviation certification body, recognised by several former ex-Soviet states, including Russia and Ukraine) with a maximum take-off weight of 392,000kg (864,212lb) and maximum payload of 120,000kg (330,693lb).

A Ruslan aircraft is equipped with two internal cranes, nose-and-tail loading with expanded ramps, and multi-leg landing gear each with 24 wheels that

An-124 Ruslan UR-82029 during the loading of an F-16 Fighting Falcon fighter jet at Tel Aviv-Ben Gurion International Airport bound for the United States. (AirTeamImages/4x6zk-moni shafir)

enable it to tilt the fuselage lower for easier loading and unloading.

All civilian-operated An-124-100s are hush-kitted and Stage 3 compliant, with up-to-date navigation and communication equipment to cope with the increasing air traffic and airport demands for higher level of flight safety during their global operations.

The An-124-100 fleet comes powered by the Ivchenko-Progress D-18T Series 3 turbofans with a maximum thrust rating of 51,654lb (229.78kN), featuring a time between overhauls of 6,000 hours (1,000 or 4,000 hours for the previous D-18T derivatives, Series 1 and 2 respectively) and a total life of 18,000 hours.

The An-124-100-150 is an enhanced version that boasts an increased payload to 150,000kg (330,693lb), while its maximum take-off weight is 402,000kg

navigator, and radio operator). There are two such aircraft, both operated by Antonov Airlines.

Once a Leader

Ulyanovsk-based Volga-Dnepr was established in 1990, initially as a commercial joint venture between several Soviet state-owned enterprises, with the main mission to support the An-124's production at Aviastar-SP and headed by Alexey Isaikin, a former deputy chief of the company's acceptance office for the Ministry of Defence of the Russian Federation. The following year it received its first Ruslan from Aviastar-SP free of charge and launched commercial operations with it in November 1991. Volga-Dnepr rapidly grew into a global business and not long afterwards the company became fully privatised, with Isaikin as the biggest shareholder.

Antonov An-124-100 Ruslan Characteristics	
Length	69.10m (226ft 8in)
Wingspan	73.30m (240ft 6in)
Height	21.08m (69ft 2in)
Wing area	628m² (6,760ft²)
Empty weight	181,000kg (399,037lb)
Max take-off weight	402,000kg (886,258lb)
Max landing weight	330,000kg (727,525lb)
Fuel capacity	210,172kg (463,343lb)
Fuel volume	262,715 lit (69,402 US gal)
Max cruise speed	467kts (865kph)
Approach speed	120–140kts (230–260kph)
Range with max payload	2,000nm (3,700km)
Range with 80,000kg payload	4,500nm (8,400km)
Range with 40,000kg payload	6,200nm (11,500km)
Ferry range with max fuel and minimum payload	7,600nm (14,000km)
Ceiling	39,000ft (12,000m)
Take-off run with max take-off weight	9,800ft (3,000m)
Landing roll with max landing weight	3,000ft (900m)
Crew	Pilot, co-pilot, navigator, chief flight engineer, electrical flight engineer, radio operator, and two loadmasters
Capacity	88 passengers in upper aft fuselage plus 350 passengers on palletised seating system
Powerplant	Four Progress D-18T high-bypass turbofan engines each rated at 51,000lbf (229kN) thrust

(886,008lb) and range is between 2,567 and 3,513nm (4,750 and 6,500km). One aircraft, c/n 01-06, was modified by Antonov in 2004, after it had logged 12,000 flight hours. The aircraft is operated by Antonov Airlines and has an extended service life of 24,000 flight hours with a self-loading capability of payloads weighing up to 40 tonnes.

The improved An-124-100M civil version features an avionics suite that enables the aircraft to be operated with a crew of four compared to a legacy jet's six-person crew (pilot, co-pilot, two flight engineers,

In the mid-1990s, Volga-Dnepr became the premier Russian cargo airline and leader in its specific niche for global transportation of super heavy and outsize cargo. It became possible thanks to the partnership with the UK company Heavylift, which offered its sales expertise in the West. The joint venture, dubbed Heavy Lift – Volga-Dnepr, was formed in 1992 and during its first year of operations the revenues accounted for $31m, growing to $102m in 1999. In 2000, however, the partners split, caused by differing views on developing the joint venture business. The American-led invasions of Afghanistan in 2001 and Iraq in 2003 led to a welcome spike in the business, as the company won lucrative contracts for transporting military cargoes. At the same time, Volga-Dnepr managed to retain and expand its customer base in the commercial world, mainly coming from the aerospace, mining, and energy sectors. By 2008, its cargo charter operations, conducted by a fleet of ten An-124s and five Il-76s, generated a revenue stream of about $1bn, with a high profit margin.

As Isaikin claimed, the An-124 is a unique aircraft for specialised operations which managed to create an entirely new segment in the aviation transport business, with nearly 90% of the company's operations outside Russia. By 2000, the An-124 hourly rate offered by Volga-Dnepr was $14,000, while in 2008 it rose to $24,000 chiefly due to the huge increase in the expenses needed for fleet maintenance, upgrades, and service life extensions.

Since the early 2010s, Volga-Dnepr has faced the serious issue of maintaining the airworthiness of its ageing and well-utilised An-124s which were subject to high utilisation – between 1,000 and 1,500 flight hours a year, with a record monthly utilisation reported in May 2010 of 300 flight hours.

By 2015, its fleet leader aircraft had racked-up 26,000 flight hours - almost half of the type's 50,000-flight hour, 45-year and 10,000 flight cycle service life as per the service life extension granted by the Antonov Design Bureau, the design authority for the type. When the An-124 was designed in the late 1970s, the Soviet

Air Force required a 16,000-flight hour, 25 year and 4,000 flight cycle service life, which was deemed as more than enough for a military transport.

Today, Volgar-Dnepr's 11 An-124's are parked-up at different locations around the world following the withdrawal of each aircraft's certificate of airworthiness by the Antonov Design Bureau following the bureau's accusation of unauthorised maintenance by the Russian operator.

Antonov Airlines

The company, established in 1989, was based in Kyiv, Ukraine. It is a fully owned subsidiary of Antonov Design Bureau (now known as Antonov State Enterprise), which that year had already requested ownership of four An-124s to use for commercial operations to support the design bureau financially. The request expressed by Antonov's long-time head, Piotr Balabuev, was satisfied by the Soviet Union's Council of Ministers. In the beginning, two aircraft were rented from the Soviet Air Force, and these were

Numerous cargo pallets on the flight line at Los Angeles International Airport during unloading from An-124 UR-82009. (AirTeamImages/John Kilmer)

immediately rushed into commercial service, generating much needed cash for Antonov. The profits from the commercial air transport business were invested in research and development activities in the 1990s and early 2000s when government funding was minimal.

Two An-124s were purchased from the Kyiv plant followed by two former Soviet Air Force machines undergoing testing at Antonov. These were considered Ukrainian property following the break-up of the Soviet Union and were added to the fleet.

Ultimately, the company's fleet gradually grew to seven aircraft and in the 2000s the operator, initially dubbed Ruslan and later renamed as Antonov Airlines, generated an annual profit of between $100m and $150m. The profits were used to keep Antonov aloft and fund the design of both the An-70 and An-140 aircraft.

Following Russia's invasion of Ukraine on February 24, 2022, five of Antonov Airline's An-124s were overseas: two at Linz in Austria, one in Nagoya, Japan, one in Guam and another in Kyrgyzstan.

Antonov Airlines' only An-124-100M-150 was at Gostomel Airport during the Russian invasion and was damaged by shelling. Its remaining five operational aircraft comprise one An-124-100, one An-124-100-150 and three An-124-100Ms.

According to the website Freight Waves, upon completion of their commercial missions Antonov Airlines' aircraft were re-positioned to Leipzig-Halle Airport, Germany, from where the airline continues operations with five An-124 aircraft.

In a statement, Antonov Airlines said: "Taking into consideration the impossibility of performing international flights from Ukraine, five An-124-100 aircraft are temporarily based at Leipzig Airport, Germany. Work by the air transport division of the Antonov Company, known in the world as the Antonov Airlines, was organised there. The technical base to provide maintenance of these aircraft also works at Leipzig airport. So, Antonov keeps the ability to perform commercial and governmental orders for transportation of superheavy and oversized cargo, as well as to retain its leading position in this niche of the world market. After victory over the Russian occupiers and restoration of the Kyiv-Antoniv-2 airport, it will again become the base for the An-124-100 fleet of Antonov Airlines."

Antonov Airlines remains one of just two internationally authorised operators of the An-124, the second is Maximus Airlines based in the UAE which has a single An-124. State-owned, Antonov Airlines can continue operations from Leipzig based on bilateral agreements between countries with individual flights taking place under seventh freedom flying privileges. Such agreements do not require a cargo service to connect to a third country.

The Ukrainian operator continues to give priority to humanitarian and military charters on behalf of the Ukrainian government and to NATO's strategic airlift programme. During the first year of enforced-exile operations from Leipzig, Antonov Airlines claimed it had spare capacity to operate 385 commercial services.

TURBO FREIGHTER

ATR has designed and built a range of turboprop airliner aircraft for over 40 years. The framer also builds freighter versions of its passenger favourites.

I f you were in the market for a turboprop in the late 1980s or early 1990s, you'd have been spoiled for choice. While the previous two decades had seen a wave of consolidation reduce the number of European and US aircraft manufacturers drastically, from 1983, at least seven airframers conducted the first flights of ten different propeller-powered products over the next decade. The crowded house would become lost in the shuffle, as manufacturers struggled to secure hard-fought orders and regional jets began to reign supreme as the millennium edged closer.

Today, just three companies – ATR, De Havilland Canada (DHC) and Embraer – remain in the turboprop game. Of those,

DHC paused Dash 8-400 production in February 2021 while Embraer is currently working on its first propeller-powered product since the EMB 120 Brasilia.

Meanwhile, across 40 years, ATR has come from obscurity to establishing itself as the go-to company for the turboprop market, with almost a monopoly.

Starting Out

ATR was formed as a joint venture and equal partnership between Aeritalia and Aerospatiale, which had both been working on regional airliner projects – the AIT 230 and AS 35, respectively. The Italian and French firms, now part of Leonardo and Airbus, respectively, originally established ATR (Aerei da

Trasporto Regionale or Avions de Transport Régional, depending on which side of the Alps you happened to be located) in October-November 1981 as a groupement d'intérêt économique under French law, with the aim of developing a family of regional airliners.

Not only had the two companies been developing their own aircraft, but they were aware that the then De Havilland Canada, British Aerospace, Saab, Embraer, Dornier, and Fokker were also vying for orders for their own 29-78 seaters.

ATR 42

The first aircraft to be produced was the ATR 42, which had its maiden flight on August 16, 1984. Certification was

ATR 72-600F Characteristics	
Length	27.17m (89ft 2in)
Width max cabin	2.57m (8ft 5in)
Wingspan	27.05m (88ft 9in)
Wing area	61.0m² (657ft²)
Height	7.65m (25ft 1in)
Max take-off weight	23,000kg (50,706lb)
Max landing weight	22,350kg (49,272lb)
Max zero fuel weight	21,000kg (46,296lb)
Operating empty weight	11,800kg (26,015lb)
Max payload	9,200kg (20,282lb)
Max fuel load	5,000kg (11,000lb)
Cabin volume	75m³ (2,124ft²)
Capacity	Five 88 x 108in or nine 88 x 62in pallets or containers, or seven LD3s
Engines	Two Pratt & Whitney Canada PW127XT-M each rated at 2,475shp (1,846kW)
Propellers	3.93m (12ft 10in) diameter, six-bladed Hamilton Standard 568F
Cruise speed with 95% max payload at 20,000ft	270kts (500kph)
Range with max payload	1,030nm (1,908km)
Ceiling	25,000ft (7,600m)
Take-off field length with MTOW at sea level	4,314ft (1,315m)
Landing distance	3,000ft (915m)
Crew	Captain and first officer

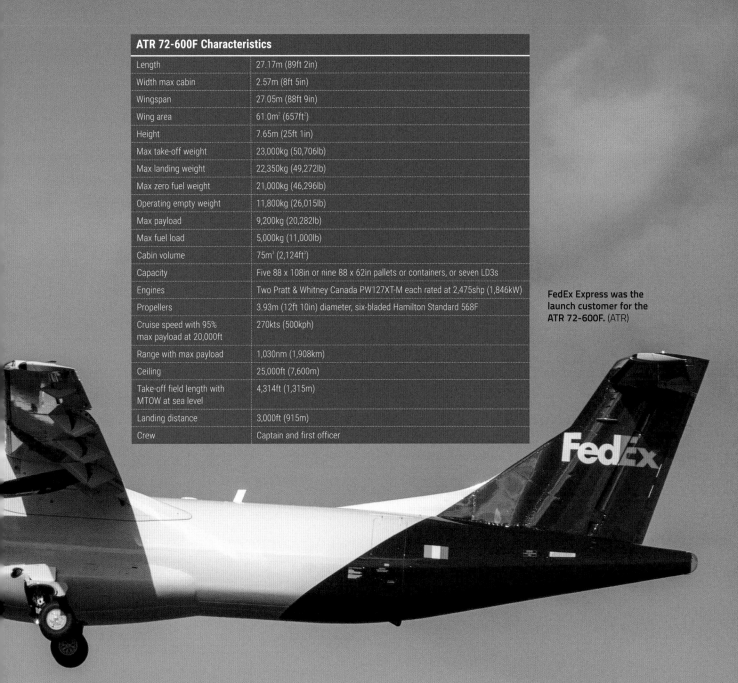

FedEx Express was the launch customer for the ATR 72-600F. (ATR)

granted by Italian and French authorities in September 1985, and the type entered service with Air Littoral – based in Le Castellet, France – on December 9, 1985. The type can carry between 42 and 50 passengers, depending on the internal fit.

Production airframes were termed the ATR 42-300, having a greater payload range and a higher take-off weight than the prototypes, while the ATR 42-320 differs in having the more powerful Pratt & Whitney Canada PW121 engines (as opposed to the standard PW120), for better hot and high performance. Other versions have included the ATR 42QC, which is a quick-change freight/passenger version of the -300 and the ATR 42 Freighter, which is a fully modified airframe for cargo use only.

ATR 72

The ATR 72 is a larger version of the original aircraft, produced to increase the seating capacity from 48 to 78 by stretching the fuselage by 15ft, increasing the wingspan, adding more powerful PW124 engines, and increasing fuel capacity by about 10%. Its design was announced in 1986, and the prototype –a converted ATR 42 – made its maiden flight on October 27, 1988. Exactly one year later, the type entered service with Finnish airline Karair, which disappeared into Finnair in 1996. Despite the ATR 42 having a two-year head start, the larger ATR 72 has proved a bigger sales success for the Franco-Italians, accounting for more than two-thirds of the 1,500+ turboprops produced since 1984.

500 Series

As more modern materials, interiors, electronics, and avionics became available, ATR decided to make improvements to its turboprops in the shape of the -500 series. The ATR 42-500 was the first significantly improved version of the aircraft and featured a revised interior, more powerful PW127E engines (for a substantially increased cruising speed) driving six-bladed propellers, a 1,000nm maximum range, the Electronic Flight Information System (EFIS) cockpit, elevators, and rudders of the stretched ATR 72 (described separately), plus new brakes and landing gear and strengthened wing and fuselage for greater weights.

The ATR 72-600F is powered by two Pratt & Whitney Canada PW127XT-M turboprop engines each rated at 2,475shp and turning a 12ft 10in diameter six-bladed Hamilton Standard 568F propellor. (ATR)

The first ATR 42-500 delivery was in October 1995, with the ATR 72-500 following two years later. The interior was completely redesigned, to create 40% more overhead baggage space and a more spacious feel to the cabin. The use of new materials and tuned vibration dampers resulted in a reduction in cabin noise and vibration – aided by the new propellers. The ATR 42-500 has a 'standard' layout that accommodates 48 passengers with a 30in seat, while the ATR 72-500 seats 68 with a 31in pitch. Both have a 90% commonality of spares, while pilots have a common type rating between the two -500 versions. This enables airlines to operate a mix of aircraft with limited additional costs.

One of the lessons learnt from earlier models resulted in the engine manufacturers, P&W, fitting a propeller brake, which enables the starboard propeller to be locked on the ground whilst the engine is still running – and therefore provide any internal power necessary. This facility – known as 'hotel mode' – has several benefits, among them obviating the need for an auxiliary power unit (APU), thus saving weight, space (and cost), plus centre of gravity considerations in placing the APU.

Piecing it Together

Major sub-assemblies of the aircraft are manufactured in France and Italy, and joined in Toulouse, from where their maiden flights are made.

Leonardo's manufacturing facilities in Pomigliano d'Arco, near Naples, Italy, produce the fuselage and tail sections, and the wings are assembled by Stelia Aerospace in Bordeaux. Other assemblies are fitted to the major parts while on the production line at Toulouse. The engines come from Pratt & Whitney Canada and the propellers arrive from Hamilton Standard in Connecticut.

From arrival at Toulouse, it takes between three and four months to complete the assembly process, ready for delivery of the finished article.

600 Series

The company received EASA type certification for the ATR 72-600 in 2011, with the ATR 42 following in mid-2012. Deliveries of the first ATR 72-600s began in August 2011, with Royal Air Maroc accepting the maiden production example, while deliveries of ATR 42-600s started in November 2012, with the first of two aircraft for Tanzania's Precision Air.

The flight deck features five wide LCD screens replacing the -500 series' electronic flight instrument system. The aircraft is powered by the up-rated PW127M engine, which has since been offered as an option on the -500, while also becoming the standard fit on the -600. It has been designed to deliver improved performance, particularly on short runways, and incorporates a boost function that provides a 5% increase in power when operating in 'hot and high' conditions.

Other Options

ATR has long offered freighters – first doing so at Farnborough in 2002. However, the Franco-Italian framer factory only converted its passenger products to cargo carriers prior to December 2020. It has since dispatched a trio of freighters to FedEx – one to ASL Airlines Ireland and the other two stateside to Empire Airlines. The US giant has ordered 30 of the custom couriers, holding options to increase its commitment to 50 examples.

Combi and Freighter Options

ATR additionally offers freighter versions of its aircraft that can be optimised for either payload or volume. The payload option, designed for bulk transportation, provides up to 6,613kg (14,579lb) of payload (ATR 42) and up to 8,904kg (19,630lb) for the ATR 72. The volume configuration, intended for rough loading operations, features a reinforced lateral panel with tracks and installation points. In this layout, the ATR 42 can carry up to 6,473kg (14,270lb) of cargo and the ATR 72 up

The ATR 72-600F measures 89ft 2in long with a wingspan of 88ft 9in. (ATR)

(ATR)

to 8,723kg (19,230lb). There is also an option of carrying industry standard LD3 containers (five in the ATR 42, seven in the ATR 72).

Freighter conversion programmes for ATR turboprop airliners have been possible from the manufacturer and third-party conversion specialists for many years, but the ATR 72-600 Freighter is the first production model to be made available. The initial ATR 72-600F, EI-GUL (c/n 1653), was handed over to FedEx Express on December 15, 2020, the first in a firm order for 30 examples, plus options for 20 more. The order was placed by the freight giant at the time of the model's launch in 2017.

Cargo Upswing

No one could have predicted the increase in demand for air cargo in 2020 due to the COVID-19 crisis. The global pandemic resulted in a huge number of emergency flights to transport medical supplies and equipment around the world, as well as greater e-commerce activity from consumers locked down at home.

Orders grew for passenger aircraft conversions to cargo use offered by third-party specialists such as Aeronautical Engineers Inc (AEI) and the Airbus-EFW joint venture, while supplementary type certificates enabled commercial aircraft

operators to repurpose passenger airliner cabins to temporarily fly as freighters.

Speaking during a virtual event to celebrate the initial ATR 72-600F handover in December 2020, Stefano Bortoli, ATR's CEO, confirmed that 11 operators had received "quick conversion solutions" to use ATR passenger aircraft as freighters.

Better Access

Jorn Van De Plas, senior vice-president Air Network and GTS Europe for FedEx Express, thinks the ATR 72-600F's introduction "marks an exciting new chapter" for the carrier. "During what has

been a difficult year both for businesses around the world and for communities, we are proud to remain at the heart of efforts to keep trade flowing and deliver goods across Europe."

All 30 FedEx ATR 72-600Fs will be operated by its partners, who fly cargo on its behalf on an aircraft, crew, maintenance, and insurance (ACMI) basis. One of those contractors is ASL Airlines, based in Shannon, Ireland which received EI-GUL and will initially operate it between Paris/CDG and the Czech Republic.

Seven ATR 72-600Fs were due for handover to FedEx in 2021, including four more for ASL and the initial examples

for FedEx's ACMI contractors in Latin America and Asia. A similar delivery rate planned for the following years means that all 30 of the aircraft in the firm order will be introduced by 2024-2025.

FedEx's operating model involves its Boeing and Airbus jets flying freight to the company's hubs, with smaller-capacity feeder aircraft then transporting goods along the regional spokes of the network. Speaking during the virtual handover event, FedEx executive vice-president and CEO Scott Struminger described the ATR 72-600F as being "a huge differentiator" for the company because it will give "better access to smaller markets" and enable it "to create

new services and ways to deliver to our customers."

The ATR 72-600F is part of FedEx's modernisation programme for its feeder fleet, and the company has also signed a deal to purchase 50 Cessna SkyCourier 408s to replace the Grand Caravans that it has been using in this role for more than 30 years. FedEx was the launch customer for the ATR 72-600F.

Connectivity

Among various enhancements recently introduced to existing ATR models is the Next Generation Multi-Function Computer (MFC NG), the latest iteration

of the aircraft's centralised computing and data communication system.

The MFC NG introduces three new applications for systems control/monitoring, maintenance tracking/fault isolation and power control, but uses the same cockpit interfaces as the MFC on earlier ATRs, so there is no crew retraining requirement.

Updated Avionics

ATRs are now delivered already fitted with the Standard 3 Avionics Suite, which includes required navigation performance with authorisation software, enabling pilots to operate at reduced minimums and follow trajectories to within 0.3-mile accuracy. The suite also features automatic dependent surveillance-broadcast-out (ADS-B) compatibility, a traffic collision and avoidance system and localiser

performance with vertical guidance. There is a satellite-based augmentation system and vertical navigation functionality coupled to the autopilot to better define descent and approach trajectories.

Automatic checklists, monitoring of terrain, traffic and weather, failure detection and pop-ups on the display screens to show appropriate procedures are further new features. Options include aircraft communications addressing and reporting, Class 2 electronic flight bag compatibility, and an airport navigation function indicating the aircraft's position on an airfield map.

ATR 72-600 Freighter

ATR launched a freighter option for the ATR 72-600 in November 2017 with a firm order for 30 aircraft from FedEx Express, plus 20 options.

The ATR 72-600F is the first cargo-configured 600-series ATR and the first ATR freighter to be delivered direct from the factory. The aircraft features a Class E freight cabin, enabling it to accommodate bulk cargo, pallets, or unit load device (ULD) containers. It has a bulk cargo capacity of 74.6m³ (2,634ft³) and can accommodate up to seven LD3 containers when in ULD configuration, or five 88 x 108in (2.2 x 2.7m) or nine 88 x 62in (2.2 x 1.5m) pallets. The aircraft has a forward large cargo door, a rear upper hinged cargo door and reinforced floor panels.

FedEx President and Chief Executive Officer David Cunningham said: "We worked with ATR to develop this new aircraft, which includes special features to help us grow our business, especially in the air freight market where shipments are larger and heavier. The ATR 72-600F

Compared to the ATR 72-600 passenger aircraft, the freighter variant has a reinforced floor, a large cargo door on the forward left side of the aircraft and no windows installed. (ATR)

will play an important role in our global network by helping us deliver fast, economical service to small and medium-sized markets."

The 2.94 x 1.8m forward fuselage cargo door surround installed to protect the aircraft while loading cargo was improved, while the cargo deck floor was reinforced for loading 1,000lb per square metre and the underfloor protection enhanced. Nine-tonne payloads can be carried using five 2.23 x 2.74m pallets or seven LD3 containers.

The ATR 72-600F was designed as a freighter from scratch, it is a 'clean' design, which reduces drag, minimises areas of potential airframe corrosion and reduces maintenance tasks. Improved onboard battery power is a further change from earlier converted ATR freighters which enables the large cargo doors to be opened and closed for two hours with enough battery power remaining to undertake the aircraft de-icing procedures until the engine is started.

Lighting output was tripled inside and outside the fuselage to ease the operator's ability to load the aircraft which often takes place at night, and to improve safety. Battery power was increased to 50 amps, enabling autonomous operation on ground without the need for a ground power unit.

Clearer View

Perhaps the most striking recent evolution on the ATR is ClearVision, designed to provide pilots with improved situational awareness in poor visibility.

Supplied by Universal Avionics, ClearVision is an enhanced vision system that uses a fuselage-mounted camera to relay high-resolution information and video in real time. The pilot wears a head-mounted, high transparency visor called Skylens to view the images.

A synthetic vision system mode provides the pilot's head-up display with digital images of terrain and obstacles, and operators can opt to have a combined vision system blending the enhanced and synthetic modes.

ClearVision-equipped aircraft can take off and land in low-visibility conditions down to 1,150ft (350m) runway visual range and 100ft (30m) decision height, making operations possible where turboprops without enhanced or synthetic systems would be unable to operate.

The ATR 72-600F's forward fuselage cargo door is 2.94m wide and 1.8m high. (ATR)

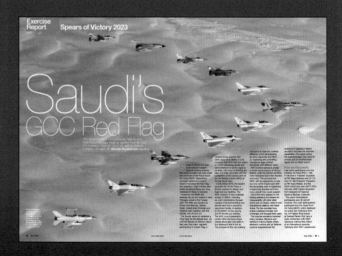

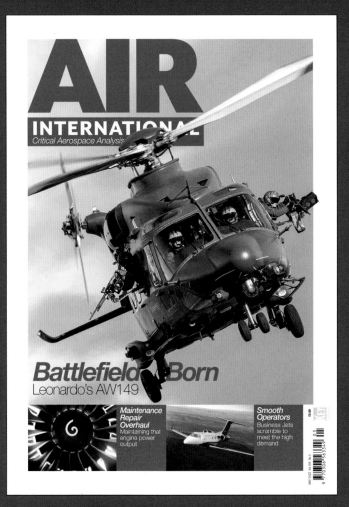

Seven-Forty-Seven Freighters

An overview of the Boeing 747 freighters which formed an important part of the success story of the legendary jumbo jet.

O ver a quarter of the world's in-service widebody freighters are Boeing 747s. In the middle of 2022 more than 260 747 freighters were in commercial service, comprising 71 747-8Fs, 152 subtypes of the 747-400F/ BCF, 35 extended-range 747-400ERFs, all four Large Cargo Freighters (LCFs) and a single 747-300SF. In addition, up to a dozen 747-200F/SFs could be operational.

Freight was integral to the design of the 747. Boeing was one of several firms that conducted studies in the mid-1960s for the US Air Force's CX-Heavy Logistics System, from which the Lockheed C-5 Galaxy strategic transport was conceived. This work provided a starting point when Juan Trippe, the legendary president of Pan American World Airways or Pan Am, asked Boeing to design an airliner to carry twice the number of passengers that could be accommodated in the 707. Boeing allocated Joe Sutter to manage the design team responsible for the new airliner, giving it the model number 747.

Of concern to Boeing was the possible short sales window for the 747. The age of the supersonic airliner was drawing near; development of the Anglo-French Concorde, the Tupolev Tu-144 and Boeing's own Model 733 (or 2707) was under way. It was feared that as soon as they entered service passengers would view subsonic travel as passé, and airlines would buy supersonic aircraft. However, cargo haulers were happier with the lower running costs of subsonic types, and so the 747 was designed for a secondary career as a large freighter. The distinctive shape of the forward fuselage, with the upper deck 'hump' behind the cockpit, created a long, main deck, which could be loaded via an upward-opening nose door or large side entrance.

Juan Trippe, on behalf of his airline, placed an order for 25 747-100s in April 1965, prior to the design being frozen. A site next to Paine Field at Everett, Washington, was acquired in mid-1966, where a huge factory to assemble 747s was built. The prototype rolled out on September 30, 1968, and test pilots Jack

Waddell and Brien Wygle, accompanied by Jess Wallick in the flight engineer's seat, took it aloft for its maiden flight on February 9, 1969. Pan Am put the 747-100 into service on January 22, 1970.

In May 1971, the US government ended funding for the 2707, then on its third major configuration. While devastating for Boeing at the time, the 2707's demise secured the future for the 747 as the emphasis shifted from speed to lower costs per seat mile.

None of the 205 747-100s were completed as freighters. The initial version was suited to US domestic operations, but additional range was needed for international routes. Boeing responded by launching the 747-200 in 1968 with a higher maximum take-off weight (MTOW), more powerful engines and longer range. It entered service in February 1971.

First Freighter

A freighter version, the 747-200F, was offered from the outset, with the nose

Boeing 747-8F flight test aircraft N747EX (c/n 35808) during its first flight in 2009. This aircraft now flies with Cargolux as LX-VCA. (Boeing)

door and optional side cargo door. A mechanical loading system allowed two people to load 242,800lb (110,132kg) of containerised or palletised cargo within 30 minutes. Up to 29 containers, each 10ft (3.05m) long, 8ft (2.44m) high and 8ft wide could be accommodated in the windowless main deck, and 30 more in the lower holds. Boeing 747-200Fs, and aircraft converted to freighters, retained the under-floor holds of the passenger variants. The hold forward of the wing could, for example, accommodate five 96 x 125 x 64in (2.44 x 3.18 x 1.63m) containers, with an additional four in the aft compartment. Each hold had its own door on the port side of the aircraft, with a third at the rear of the aft hold for up to 800ft³ (22.6m³) of bulk cargo.

The 747-200F could fly 200,000lb (90,718kg) over 4,500nm (8,336km).

The first 747-200F N79713 (c/n 20373) flew on November 30, 1971 and launch customer Lufthansa Cargo received its initial example on March 9, 1972. They went on to order five more singularly, the last on May 27, 1987. Of the 393 747-200s

built, 73 were freighters for 21 airlines, with Air France and Northwest Airlines (both taking eight), Japan Airlines (seven), Flying Tigers, Lufthansa, and Nippon Cargo Airlines (all with six) among major purchasers. The final 747-200F (for Nippon Cargo Air Lines) was delivered on November 19, 1991.

Boeing began working on a passenger-to-freighter conversion for the 747-100

and 747-200 in 1972, receiving an initial Supplemental Type Certificate (STC) from the Federal Aviation Administration (FAA) in 1974. The major structural change involved the installation of a 10ft 3in (3.12m) high and 11ft 2in (3.40m) wide side cargo door on the port side of the fuselage. Other modifications included removal of all passenger seats and furnishings,

The nose cargo door is one of the 747 Freighter's distinguishing features. (Boeing)

Boeing delivered the 16th and last 747-400F to Cargolux on July 25, 2008. The Luxembourg carrier took delivery of its first 747 Freighter in 1978. (Boeing)

The 747's future operation is as a high-capacity cargo aircraft. Cargolux uses 14 747-8 Freighters, including LX-VCB (c/n 35806). (Boeing)

strengthening the main deck floor, addition of tie-downs for freight and a two-man cargo handling system. Conversions, known as Special Freighters, lacked the swing nose of production 747-200Fs, but still carried 29 pallets on the main deck. Aircraft modified from 747-100s had a maximum structural payload weight of 210,200lb (95,345kg), and 747-200 conversions 238,900lb (108,363kg).

In 1983 Pan Am agreed to modify 19 of its passenger-configured 747s (15 747-100s and four 747-200s) assigned to the US Civil Reserve Air Fleet (CRAF), with an aft cargo door added and other changes. CRAF aircraft are made available to the US Department of Defense only in times of emergency and the 747s remained the property of Pan Am. The agreement was the first of its kind and the US military designation C-19A was allocated for contractual purposes. The first, Clipper Sea Serpent (N665PA, c/n 20350), was redelivered following modification on May 31, 1985, and the last in February 1990.

Special Freighter conversion kits were produced by Boeing at its Wichita, Kansas facility, and conversions were either undertaken there or customers could choose another facility to perform the work. For example, Taikoo (Xiamen) Aircraft Engineering Co (TAECO) based at Gaoqi International Airport in China, completed its first 747-200 conversion in 2000. By early 1985, 25 freighters had been redelivered; this had increased to 90 by 2000, although this also includes

Boeing 747-8F N747EX (b/n RC501) made the type's first flight from Everett-Paine Field, Washington on February 8, 2010, initiating a six-month flight-test programme. (Boeing)

Only 81 747-300s were delivered, and none as freighters. The most significant change was the Stretched Upper Deck (SUD), increasing the length of the distinctive forward bulge by 23ft 4in (7.11m), more than doubling the number of passengers in that section. Swissair put the first 747-300 into passenger service on March 28, 1983, but the variant was quickly replaced by the 747-400 on the production line.

In May 2000 Boeing announced a freighter conversion programme for the 747-300, following a launch order for three combi-to-freighters from Atlas Air. Based on the 747-200 Special Freighter, converted 747-300s had the same internal volume (26,600ft³/753m³) as the 747-200F

modifications to combi (mixed passenger/cargo) configurations.

Boeing was not the only company to offer such conversions. Pemco of Florida developed a passenger-to-freighter package for the 747-100, which included a 10ft 3in (3.12m) by 11ft 5in (3.48m) cargo door fitted on the port side aft of the wing; cabin windows were blanked out; an electric cargo handling system installed; a 9g bulkhead added behind the flight deck and the upper deck was reconfigured. The aircraft could carry up to 202,000lb (91,626kg) of cargo. An FAA STC was granted in April 1988 and six conversions were completed by April 1991.

Israel Aircraft Industries' (IAI) Bedek Aviation Group also developed a freighter conversion for 747-200s, at Ben Gurion International Airport, Tel Aviv, redelivering its first to Lufthansa in August 1990. Like other conversions, a main deck cargo door was installed aft of the wing of the port side, while the area around it and the flooring was reinforced, and a powered ball mat/roller cargo handling and restraint system installed. Bedek completed 38 conversions by the end of 2005, returning its final example to Northwest Airlines early in 2006. By then, IAI was working on a similar programme for the 747-400, for which it had sold out slots until 2009.

The five-aircraft 747-8F test fleet completed more than 1,200 flights and 3,400 hours since the first flight and gathered data for more than 1,700 FAA certification requirements. (Boeing)

The Boeing 747-8F undertook flight-test operations at the Southern California Logistics Airport, also known as Victorville Airport in Southern California. The Boeing 747-8F successfully completed its certification flight test programme on August 2, 2011, when test aircraft RC522 and RC523 landed at Everett-Paine Field. RC522 completed testing of the flight management computer and RC523 completed function and reliability testing: the final phase in which an aircraft must accrue 300 FAA-approved flight hours in its final delivery configuration. (Boeing)

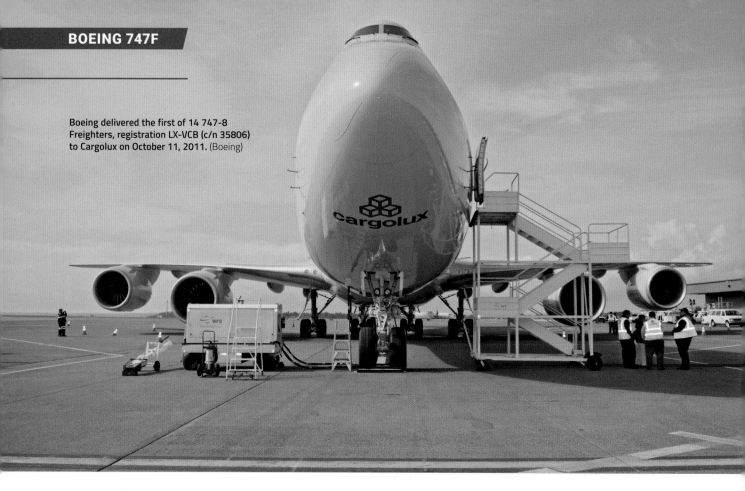

Boeing delivered the first of 14 747-8 Freighters, registration LX-VCB (c/n 35806) to Cargolux on October 11, 2011. (Boeing)

and could transport 235,000lb (106,594kg) some 4,200nm (7,781km).

Only six 747-300 Special Freighters were produced. The first completed in October 2000 went to Atlas Air. It was eventually acquired by TCA of Georgia, which sold it (as EW-465TQ) to Transaviaexport Cargo in May 2016, and is the last 747-300 in service. Atlas also had a second, while one served with Korean Air. TAECO modified at least two former Singapore Airlines aircraft that were delivered to Dragonair in 2001, while the Hong Kong-based carrier received a third from Boeing in April 2002.

Boeing 747-400F

New technology engines, advanced materials, improved aerodynamics, and systems made the 747-400 a significant improvement on earlier variants. In passenger form, it retained the Stretched Upper Deck (SUD) of the 747-300, had longer, strengthened wings with large winglets, carried more fuel and had carbon brakes. The introduction of a glass cockpit removed the need for a flight engineer.

A freighter variant was planned from the outset. Visible differences included the omission of the cabin windows and the SUD, which would have reduced the height of the forward main deck by approximately two feet (0.6m) limiting the types of containers that could be carried. Structural weight was also reduced by 4,410lb (2,000kg) by incorporating advanced

materials, raising the payload capability to 249,125lb (113,001kg) which could be flown 4,400nm (8,143km). The 747-400F retained the nose cargo door of the 747-200F, with the option of the port rear side cargo door, to accommodate up to 30 pallets on the 21,350ft³ (605m³) main deck, which was lined with motor driven rollers. There was 5,600ft³ (159m³) of space in the under-floor cargo hold, in which, for example, 32 LD-1 containers could be stowed. A further 520ft³ (15m³) was available for bulk cargo in another under-floor hold accessed via its own door on the rear fuselage.

Loading time was reduced, thanks to an improved freight handling system.

Prototype 747-428F N6005C rolled out at Everett on March 8, 1993, and first flew on May 4. Certification by the FAA was granted on October 27, 1993, after a brief flight test campaign, building on that undertaken for the 747-400. Launch customer Air France ordered five in 1989, but never received them, changing its commitment to the combi (400M) version. It was Cargolux of Luxembourg that took delivery of the first 747-400F (the second built) on November 17, 1993; it also acquired the prototype in September 1995.

In service, the 747-400F demonstrated a 15% lower fuel burn per pound of payload than the 747-200F. The combination of

Cargolux used the aircraft's nose-door cargo loading capability for its first revenue service October 12, 2011. The Boeing 747-8F has a maximum structural payload capacity of 133.9 tonnes. (Boeing)

Swiss-based Panalpina Welttransport Holding AG operated two Boeing 747-8 Freighters, N850GT (c/n 37570) and N851GT (c/n 37565), for a few years until the company ceased operations in 2020. (Boeing)

payload and reduced operating costs, plus a growth in air cargo traffic, helped drive sales. Boeing produced 126 with its biggest customer, China Airlines, taking 21, followed by Singapore Airlines (17), Cargolux (16), Atlas Air (15), Korean Air and Nippon Cargo Airlines (10 each). A single 747-400F was acquired by the US Air Force and heavily modified as the YAL-1A Airborne Laser (ABL) with a chemical oxygen iodine laser occupying the main deck. The ABL project was cancelled in December 2011. The 747-400F was also allocated the US military designation – C-33A – when it was studied as a Non-Developmental Airlift Aircraft to complement the C-17A Globemaster III.

Qantas' commitment for six 747-400ERs launched the programme for this variant on November 28, 2000. Structural modifications and a stronger landing gear allowed a heavier weight of 910,000lb (412,769kg) and more fuel to fly 435nm (805km) further than the 747-400. The Australian airline, the only customer, received its first on October 31, 2002. Boeing had quickly identified the improvements would be good for a freighter and announced the 747-400ERF on April 30, 2001, following an order placed 13 days earlier by International Lease Finance Corporation. Compared with the 747-400F it could carry 22,000lb (9,979kg) more and for 280nm (525km) further.

Prototype N5017Q rolled out on September 5, 2002, and completed its maiden flight on September 30. FAA approval was given on October 16 and Air France took delivery of

Cathay Pacific Cargo operates a fleet of 14 747-8 Freighters. Aircraft B-LJK (c/n 43394) was delivered on December 18, 2013, the first 747-8 equipped with performance-improved GEnx-2B engines as part of the aircraft's Performance Improvement Package. (Boeing)

the first the following day. Forty were built for ten customers.

Boeing delivered 694 of the 747-400 variant, including 166 747-400F/ERF freighters. The last new-build 747-400F was delivered to Nippon Cargo Airlines on May 7, 2009. Delivery of two 747-400ERFs for LoadAir Cargo of Kuwait directly into desert storage on November 10, 2009, concluded 747-400 production. The latter carrier never started operations and one of the aircraft joined Michigan-based Kalitta Air in 2011 and the other Cargolux in 2013.

In 2000 Boeing began design of a Special Freighter conversion package for the 747-400, and formally launched the programme in January 2004, following receipt of an initial order for six (plus six options) from Cathay Pacific. To distinguish it from similar rival projects, it was being marketed as the Boeing Converted Freighter (BCF) by the time the FAA approved the Major Design Change on December 13, 2005.

The 747-400BCF retained the extended upper deck of the passenger variant,

United Parcel Service took delivery of its 28th and final Boeing 747-8F, registration N633UP (c/n 65774) in April 2022. (Boeing)

although reconfigured as a crew rest area for eight or (optionally) 19 occupants. A freight door, supplied by Mitsubishi Heavy Industries, was installed on the rear of the port side while most of the cabin windows were blanked out. The main deck could accommodate up to 30 pallets, for a total payload capability of 250,000lb (113,398kg), which could be flown 4,085nm (7,564km).

Boeing chose to outsource conversion of the aircraft to three approved companies. TAECO was responsible for the initial customer aircraft, which was delivered to Cathay Pacific in December 2005. KAL Aerospace, a division of Korean Air, completed all but one of 20 conversions for that airline at its Gimhae facility. The initial conversions by SIA Engineering of Singapore were four former Singapore Airlines' 747-400s for Dragonair.

Pan American World Airways Boeing 747-121(A-SF) N655PA 'Clipper Sea Serpent'. (Wikipedia)

747-8F Fleet	
Operator	**Orders**
Air Bridge Cargo	12
Air Belgium	3
Atlas Air	8
Cargolux	14
Cathay Pacific Cargo	14
Korean Air Cargo	7
Nippon Cargo Airlines	8
Polar Air Cargo	6
Qatar Airways	2
Silk Way Airlines	5
UPS Airlines	28
Total	**107**
Data: Boeing	

In September 2002, IAI also announced the 747-400 Bedek Special Freighter (BDSF) modification programme by its Bedek Aviation Group. In addition to the standard addition of a large freight door, floor strengthening, other adaptations for cargo and reconfiguring the interior of the SUD, the floor beams of the upper deck were removed to allow 10ft (3m) containers on the forward main deck. Up to 253,575lb (115,020kg) could be flown over 4,000nm (7,400km) by the 747-400BDSF.

IAI predicted a worldwide requirement for 300 converted freighters; it aimed to account for 40% of that number, with a capacity of completing 16 per year. Guggenheim Aviation Partners became the launch customer with two former Air Canada combis becoming full freighters.

The first was delivered to Air China Cargo on August 1, 2006. That year Asiana ordered conversions of three combis (plus three options) as freighters, which were redelivered in 2007; an option was firmed and delivered in 2010. The final conversion at Ben Gurion was redelivered in 2012 and at the time was believed to be the last.

Several factors conspired to limit the number of 747-400 modifications. The global economic downturn from September 2008 had a significant impact. Rising fuel costs, over capacity, a weakening travel market and a new generation of passenger twins – such as the Boeing 777 and Airbus A330 – meant second-hand 747-400s were available, which for a period boosted freighter conversion replacements of older aircraft. As the dedicated air cargo market diminished and more was transported in the holds of passenger aircraft, older generation widebody freighters became economic liabilities.

With 747-400Fs entering storage, few carriers would pay to modify old airliners.

Boeing announced the official end of the BCF programme in October 2016. None had been delivered since the summer of 2012. The BCF and BDSF programmes involved a total of 81 aircraft, including around 32 in Israel, well short of initial expectations. Surprisingly, in 2016 Asiana firmed up its final BDSF options, the work to convert the combis (already fitted with the side cargo door) to all-freight configuration being cheaper than a used 747-400F. The first was completed in April 2016, by which time the second was being worked on.

When Boeing investigated transporting large sub-sections of its 787 Dreamliner between production sites around the globe, it chose a similar solution to that adopted by its arch rival. Airbus had long employed outsized transporters – Aero Spacelines Super Guppies then A300-600ST Belugas – to move parts around its dispersed facilities. Boeing proposed to do the same with the Large Cargo Freighter (LCF) conversion of the 747-400.

A promotional photo for the first Lufthansa 747-200 Freighter in 1972. (Boeing)

Evergreen Aviation Technologies of Taoyuan, Taiwan, was contracted to modify four pre-used aircraft. An enlarged upper fuselage section was designed, while Gamesa Aeronautica of Spain developed a hinged swing-tail so that cargo could be loaded from the rear. To retain directional stability, disrupted by the bulged fuselage, the height of the fin was increased by five feet (1.52m).

In 1972, Boeing used this photo to demonstrate how much 'stuff' the new 747-200 Freighter could carry. (Boeing)

Lufthansa's first 747 Freighter, D-ABYE (c/n 20373) in a 1972 promotional image demonstrating its nose-door cargo loading capability. (Boeing)

The first rolled out on August 17, 2006, and flew on September 9. Boeing conducted the initial mission carrying Dreamliner parts on January 15, 2007, by when the LCF had been christened the Dreamlifter.

On June 2, 2007, Evergreen International Airlines took over the flight operations of the variant from Boeing. All four had been completed by February 2010. After Evergreen went out of business, Atlas Air was awarded the contract in September 2010.

Studies for improved 747s continued throughout the 2000s, with later concepts incorporating technology developed for the Dreamliner. These crystallised around the 747 Advanced, which was formally launched as the 747-8 on November 14, 2005. Approximately 70% of structural components differed from the 747-400, including new engines (General Electric GEnx-2B67s); higher gross weight and an 18ft 4in/5.6m longer fuselage, to 250ft 2in/76.25m. It also had a redesigned wing with raked tips in place of winglets giving a larger wingspan. Passenger (747-8

Intercontinental) and freighter (747-8F) versions were designed. The latter retained the earlier variants' nose cargo door and rear port side loading door. It featured a windowless cabin, freight handling systems and a short upper deck compared with the 747-8I. Payload increased to 34 pallets on the main deck. Initial orders were ten for Cargolux, and eight for Nippon Cargo Airlines.

Boeing 747-8F

Prototype 747-8F N747EX rolled out on November 12, 2009, and was flown on February 8, 2010. A 3,400-hour flight test campaign ended with the 747-8F being awarded joint FAA and European Aviation Safety Agency approval on August 19, 2011. Boeing planned the initial delivery to Cargolux for September 19, 2011, but a contractual dispute between the two delayed acceptance until October 12.

The 747-8F has a cavernous 30,288ft³ (857m³) volume with 34 positions for 8 x 10ft (2.4 x 3m) contoured pallets on

the main deck and 12 positions on the lower deck, where there is also space for two additional LD-1 or LD-3 containers. Cargolux quotes a maximum revenue payload of 295,000lb (134,000kg).

As well as high capacity, the 747-8F offers operational flexibility, thanks to the multiple loading points: the distinctive upwards-rotating nose cargo door and the main deck side cargo doors on either side of the rear fuselage.

The aircraft serves the higher-capacity end of the air cargo market and only so many airlines require an aircraft of the 747-8F's capacity. Most of the major cargo specialists put the 747-8F into service in numbers to meet their respective requirements. With those requirements met, the prospect for further sales were limited. An added pressure to the 747-8F's commercial prospects was the market trend for efficient twinjet widebody cargo aircraft such as the 777 Freighter and a ready feedstock of older medium-sized twin jets creates opportunities for freighter conversions.

First flight of Cargolux Boeing 747-400F LX-FCV (c/n 25866) in late 1993, its first 400-series freighter. (Boeing)

Not even the 747-8F is protected from the twin-jet tide, even though it fills a valuable niche in air cargo thanks to its huge capacity. Boeing's Commercial Market Outlook predicted the share of the market held by large widebody freighters such as 747-8Fs and converted 747-400s will decline from 29% to 25% over the next two decades, while the fleet share of medium-sized freighters like 777Fs will grow by 3%.

On January 12, 2021, Atlas Air ordered four 747-8Fs which were the final four 747s built. The final aircraft, a 747-8F produced as line number 1574 (the 1,574th 747 built), rolled off the Everett production line on December 6, 2022, and was delivered to Atlas Air on January 31, 2023. Boeing sold 107 747-8Fs in all.

Combi Variants

Boeing produced several different combi variants of the 747 in addition to the pure freighters. Combi aircraft offer airlines the flexibility to carry purely passengers, freight, or a mix of both. In the early days of the 747 carriers struggled to fill the airliner, and combi variants allowed them to fly routes that passenger numbers could not justify. They could also help airlines alleviate problems caused by seasonal peaks and troughs in the passenger and air freight markets by changing the ratio of seating to freight or reconfiguring the aircraft for one use or the other. In contrast to the passenger configuration, combi versions included a side loading cargo door installed aft of the wing on the port side, a removable bulkhead to separate passengers and cargo on the main deck and some structural strengthening.

Boeing's first variant to combine the two payloads, the 747-200C Convertible, had the nose freight door of the true freighter (a feature lacking in later combi variants), while the side loading door was optional. The 747-200C could be used for all-passenger or cargo operations, or any of five mixed configurations. It first flew on March 23, 1973, and World Airways received the initial example on April 27 that year. Just 13 were built.

The first true combis were a pair of Sabena 747-129s modified with a side loading door; the initial 747-129(M) was redelivered to the Belgian airline in February 1974. Production combi variants were the 747-200M, 747-300M and 747-400M, based on corresponding passenger versions, of which 78, 21 and 61 respectively were delivered. On March 7, 1975, Air Canada accepted the first 747-200M. The model proved popular in Europe, with Lufthansa (14), Air France (11) and KLM (7) acquiring the largest fleets direct from the manufacturer, allowing them to fly 747s on routes that passenger numbers alone would have dictated the use of smaller types. As general air traffic continued to grow during the 1980s and 1990s, the need for new combi 747s declined as the airline industry increasingly segmented into dedicated passenger operations or freight operations.

While nearly a fifth of the 747-200s built were 747-200Ms, less than a tenth of the total production of 747-400 jumbos comprised 747-400Ms.

Cargolux Boeing 747-400F LX-FCV (c/n 25866) parked on the flight line at Everett-Paine Field. (Boeing)

DHL Air Boeing 757-200SF G-BMRA
(c/n 23710) at East Midlands Airport.
(AirTeamImages/Enda Burke)

Cargo King

A growing number of Boeing 757 freighters serve the worlds cargo carriers. Jon Lake charted the evolutionary course of this flexible freighter for *Air International* magazine.

The Boeing 757 was designed as a replacement for the older Model 727, and it was perhaps inevitable that Boeing's new narrow-body would follow its trijet predecessor into the cargo market. Although wide-bodied aircraft were rapidly being pressed into use in the freighter role, especially on intercontinental routes, and though these were enjoying great popularity thanks to their capacious cabins, there was still a place for smaller freighters to provide capacity along 'the spokes' that emanated from the cargo carriers' regional hubs. And the 757 promised to do so while offering much better fuel economy than the 727, and with the ability to use shorter or hot and high runways.

757-200PF

Thus, just four years and nine months after Eastern Air Lines had put the passenger-carrying 757-200 into commercial service on January 1, 1983,

optimised for freight, and the aircraft has a smaller cockpit compared to passenger variants. To access this a smaller crew entry door for the pilots was added near the cockpit windows, In place of the normal forward boarding door. The new crew entry door is "better described as a hatch," according to one pilot, who said that "it's a bit of a squeeze to get into the pilot seats. But once strapped in, it's pure Boeing 757!"

Only 80 aircraft were built as freighters on the Renton production line, but many more have been converted to freighter or combi standards by a number of companies, including Boeing itself.

Some 75 of the Boeing-built 757 freighters were delivered to UPS (with whom they remain in service), the first being Boeing 757-24APF N401UP (line number 139). All were powered by Pratt & Whitney PW2040 engines. The aircraft was delivered to United Parcel Service (UPS) on October 6, 1987, and was pressed into service to deliver packages at night, loaded onto pallets or LD3 containers.

The Boeing 757-200PF has a total payload of 40 tonnes for medium-haul flights and can carry bulk goods with a volume of approximately 50m³. The aircraft is equipped with an auxiliary power unit for long-haul flights.

The next operator of the 757-200PF was Challenge Air Cargo, which took delivery of three Rolls Royce RB211-535E4 powered aircraft from July 26, 1989, using the designation Boeing 757-23APF. The aircraft were leased from Ansett Worldwide – whose fourth 757-23APF initially went to Zambian Airlines. The next 757-200PF operator was Ethiopian Airlines, who would operate two dedicated freighter examples of the 757, powered by Pratt and Whitney PW2040 engines, alongside a dozen passenger versions. The first of these was a new-build 757-260PF, ET-AJS (line number 300), which joined Ethiopian on August 24, 1990. This made Ethiopian the first passenger-carrying airline to order and receive the freighter version of the 757. The aircraft served until June 2018, and remains in use with Asia Pacific Airlines.

The second Ethiopian 757 freighter was originally delivered as a passenger-configured aircraft in February 1991, serving the airline for 15 years before conversion to freighter configuration in 2006. It then flew cargo for Ethiopian for more than a decade, finally being withdrawn in October 2017.

The three aircraft delivered to Challenge Air Cargo served until late 1999/early

the Boeing 757-200PF package freighter variant entered service with UPS in September 1987 and the 757-200M combi model followed suit with Nepal Airlines in September 1988.

The 757-200PF variant has a maximum take-off weight of 255,000lb (115,666kg) and a maximum range of 3,150nm (5,830km). In practise, this means that the 757-200PF can carry a maximum 86,900lb (39,417kg) load on the 6,600ft³ (187m³) main deck, swallowing up to 15 standard-sized (15 x 25in/381 x 635mm) containers. Loading and unloading is undertaken using an upward-opening freight door in the forward part of the fuselage on the port side just ahead of the wing. The main deck is augmented by two lower deck holds (one forward of the wings, one aft) providing a further 1,830ft³ (51.8m³) of space for bulk cargo.

The aircraft was built with most of the doors and windows of the passenger version omitted. The floor plan of the 757-200PF is

Boeing 757-200SF N967FD (c/n 26269) is one of 113 currently in service with FedEx Express. The jet is seen at San Jose Airport in Costa Rica. (AirTeamImages/Jose Salazar)

2000, and all found new operators in the shape of Icelandair, SNAS Aviation, and European Air Transport.

The second Challenge aircraft went on to fly with Cameroon Airlines, Ansett, Icelandair, Arrow Air, and others, finally ending up with Spain's Swiftair. The third aircraft has served mainly with different DHL partner carriers and remains in use with DHL Air Austria.

Two Boeing 757-29JAPF aircraft for Egypt's Shorouk Air were, in the end, not taken up.

The 757-24APF is now in its 35th year of operation with UPS, but the aircraft are being upgraded for continued service, receiving a Collins Aerospace (formerly Rockwell Collins) and Boeing-designed flight deck upgrade. This will see six obsolescent cathode ray tube (CRT) displays being replaced by more reliable large-format (15.1in) LCD screens. Much the same upgrade is being applied to the carrier's Boeing 767s (which share a common type rating with the 757).

Captain Ken Hoke, a UPS Airlines Boeing 757 and 767 pilot, told *AIR International* that: "The Collins LDS is intuitive. After only a few flights, I prefer the LDS cockpit; and our flight crews will soon enjoy the benefits on every flight. I may be a fan of antiques, but I won't miss the classic Seven-Five instrument panel. "Initial pilot reaction to the large-format display system [LDS] flight deck upgrade was very positive. Although the classic cockpits are well liked, crew members who previously flew more modern equipment missed the benefits of advanced displays. Those of us raised on older 'steam gauges' were excited about the new features available with LDS," Hoke said. "As more aircraft are converted, maintaining currency is easier. "For an old-timer like me, the first few flights in an LDS aircraft were

a fun challenge. LDS provides more information to the pilots. And it's all good info. Speed tapes, trend vectors, improved traffic collision and avoidance system [TCAS] guidance, flight path vectors, and more, improve situational awareness. All this new data requires a different visual scan. It takes time and concentration to adapt."

Conversions

The 80 new build 757-200PFs and a single Combi 757-200M have been augmented by about 317 aircraft (so far) converted to freighter or Combi standards from 757-200 airliners. These passenger to freighter (P2F) conversions have been undertaken by a range of engineering companies – including Boeing itself.

There were three main Supplementary Type Certificates (STCs) covering 757 freighter conversions, resulting in slightly different aircraft configurations, though all start by adding a cargo door on the port forward fuselage (identical to that fitted to the new-build 757-200PF), and by removing all passenger amenities. Most cabin doors are sealed shut, and cabin windows are deleted.

The original Boeing STC covered the original 757-200SF conversion – beginning with the 29 former British Airways 757-236s converted to 757SF standards at Wichita and Tel Aviv/Ben Gurion for DHL. Five of these remain in service.

The Boeing STC was sold to IAI in conjunction with Singapore Technologies (ST Aero)/Mobile Aerospace (MAE) and was subsequently refined and improved.

The second STC was developed by Alcoa/SIE and resulted in the 14Plus B757-200ASF configuration. This STC was subsequently acquired by Pemco World Air Services in Tampa, Florida.

Confusingly, both Boeing/IAE/ST Aero/ Mobile Aerospace and Alcoa/Pemco conversions tend to be designated as 757-200SFs (Special Freighters).

The final 757 freighter STC was held by Precision Conversions (later Precision Aircraft Solutions), with the 757-200PCF – initially distinguished by being the first conversion able to carry 15 pallets, rather than 14 or 14.5.

The difference is primarily a product of door configuration – those conversions that retain the normal L1 entrance door had 14 positions for 125 x 88 pallets or ULD (unit load device) containers – sometimes with an additional 'half-size' 88x88 pallet in Position A. Optionally, the 757SF could accommodate 12 125 x 96in pallets by moving quick-release locks from the 88in to the 96in position.

Those conversions that removed the L1 door, and replaced it with a smaller, inward opening crew entry hatch, (like that of the production 727-200PF) recouped useful weight savings, reduced maintenance requirements, and gained

a full (15th) pallet position in Position A, more than justifying the expense of removing the entry door! The 757 freighter frequently ran out of space well before they reached their payload weight limit, so an extra pallet position was especially useful. The only downside, according to one pilot, was that the toilet was now on the flight deck.

Partners

Boeing undertook freighter conversions in association with a number of partners, including ST Aero and IAI (for aircraft destined for DHL), and ST Aero alone (for aircraft destined for FedEx).

Singapore Technologies Engineering, or ST Aero, then claimed to be the "world's largest commercial airframe MRO provider," and engaged in passenger-to-freighter conversions for many years, principally as a provider of touch labour for Boeing rather than as a developer of its own conversion programmes. This began to change in 2007 when ST Aero signed a deal with FedEx for 87 (later 119)

Boeing 757-200SF freighters, these featuring a 14-pallet configuration. ST (through its subsidiary VT Mobile Aerospace Engineering, Inc.) delivered the last of these aircraft in mid-2015. VT MAE was established in September 1990 by ST Engineering and is located at Brookley Aeroplex in Mobile, Alabama, and at the Pensacola International Airport in Pensacola, Florida.

ST Aero's contract for 119 conversions for FedEx means that the company has converted more 757-200s to freighter configuration than any of its competitors. But almost all of those were aircraft configured to carry 14 pallets, and so, as the end of the contract approached ST Aerospace began work on certification of its own 15-pallet conversion. In early 2016, ST Aero received certification for a 15-pallet 757-200 P-to-F conversion and delivered five conversions to launch customer SF Airlines from 2018.

Another 757 freighter STC was granted to Alcoa-SIE Cargo Conversions' (ASCC), which produced its first '14Plus' 757-200SF conversion for Babcock & Brown Aircraft Management in 2005. The aircraft was delivered from the

United Parcel Services currently operates 75 Boeing 757-200PFs including N454UP (c/n 25475) seen at Miami.
(AirTeamImages/Steven Marquez)

conversion facility - Commercial Jet, Inc. at Miami International Airport in Miami, Florida, a sister company of Aeronautical Engineers, Inc. (AEI), in January 2007. The 14Plus configuration was claimed to offer 97% of the pallet volume of the 15-pallet configuration (and equal payload weight) at 80% of the cost.

ASCC's 14Plus offered a simpler design that retained more of the Boeing 757-200's original structure and systems, thereby significantly reducing conversion time and cost while retaining an area for Supernumeraries, three coach class seats, a full galley and lavatory.

In 2010, the 757 cargo conversion operations and assets of Alcoa-SIE Conversions (ASCC) were acquired by Pemco World Air Services, and thereafter were marketed as a Pemco product. ASCC president Robert Murphy noted that the 757 freighter would "round out the product portfolio in the Pemco family of narrowbody cargo aircraft options," and said that he was "pleased to see the highly efficient conversion design that ASCC has pioneered incorporated into the product line of one of the world's most experienced cargo conversion companies."

757-200PCF

In 2001 Oregon-based Erickson Air-Crane created Precision Conversions as a new, standalone business to undertake the engineering, prototyping, and certification of a new 15-pallet 757-200 passenger-to-freighter conversion programme – the Boeing 757-200PCF.

The new version featured a Class E cargo compartment with a reinforced floor structure, a seven-track ANCRA cargo handling system, and a rigid 9G barrier. The aircraft was able to carry 15 88 x 125in or 88 x 108in pallets or 13 larger 96 x 125in pallets or containers on the main deck. The flight deck had seating for up to six and a new crew lavatory installation.

Precision claims that the B757-200PCF is the market leader with the lowest operating empty weight (115,500–116,000lb) and the highest available payload (up to 84,000lb) of any 757-freighter conversion. This makes it 1,500–1,800lb lighter than the competition, and Precision offers additional significant optional weight upgrades.

The Precision B757-200PCF has been certified by the FAA, and EASA, and in Brazil, Canada, China, and Russia, with over 153 delivered and 134 in active service around the world.

The 757-freighter proved popular as a replacement for the trijet Boeing 727 and the four-engine DC-8 aircraft, offering higher capacity and greatly improved fuel efficiency. The 757 has been particularly relevant to the European market because of its capacity and range but has also been heavily used in the United States and China.

In late 2021, *Aviation Business News* reported that the Boeing 757-200 continued to be the "pre-eminent candidate for conversion" in the large narrow body segment, though *Air Cargo News* noted the emergence of a new rival. It pointed out that although ten aircraft had been converted in 2020, with eight more in 2021, and an additional 30 due to be converted in the future, "conversions of the Airbus A321-200 are now growing with three so far in 2021, three in 2020, and with a further 19 set to be converted in the future." This could suggest that the 757 will soon lose its crown as King of the narrow body freighters.

Boeing 777 Freighters

Boeing took a gamble on the market being ready for a new-build freighter version of the 777 and gained considerable success.

The Boeing 777 is the largest twin-jet airliner ever produced. From its October 1990 launch to the time of writing in March 2023, a total of 2,141 examples had been ordered, of which 1,702 had been delivered.

Six Triple Seven variants have entered service to date: the 777-200, the 777-200ER, the 777-300, the 777-300ER, the ultra-long-range 777-200LR and the 777 Freighter. Two new variants, the 777-8 and 777-9, are currently under development in the 777X programme launched in 2013. The first 777-9 made the variant's maiden flight on January 25, 2020, and following delays in certification, service entry is currently expected in 2025.

Boeing has sold 88 777-200s, 60 777-300s, 422 777-200ERs, 61 777-200LRs and 319 777Fs. The 777Xs have secured 353 orders so far.

In response to requests from some of Boeing's most important customers, in 2004 the manufacturer set up a working group involving 20 airlines and cargo operators, with a view to designing and producing an all-freight version of the Boeing 777. It was envisaged as a replacement for cargo versions of the McDonnell Douglas DC-10 and MD-11, and Boeing 747, 757 and 767 freighters. A launch order from Air France for five 777Fs in May 2005 got the ball rolling, with the type's inaugural flight taking place on July 14, 2008. The first example was delivered on February 19 the following year to Air France.

The 777F can carry a 242,500lb payload and has a maximum take-off weight of 766,000lb. Twenty-seven standard pallets can be accommodated on the main deck, with space for ten more in the lower cargo hold. Additionally, there is room

for 600ft³ of bulk freight in the aft belly hold. It can accommodate various types and sizes of pallets. Many cargo operators carry bloodstock, usually horses being transported between race meetings in different countries or being brought to and from stud. For these operations, there is a small section known as the supernumerary area near the forward door that can be used by handlers. It has four business-sized seats, a galley and toilet facilities plus two bunks.

With a max payload range of 5,400nm the aircraft can fly further than the 747-8F. The aircraft includes features of the 777-200LR, marketed as the Worldliner,

(Boeing)

such as the basic airframe and engines, but incorporates the fuel capacity of the larger 777-300ER.

Standard features from across the 777 series include a state-of-the-art flight deck, fly-by-wire controls and an advanced wing design that includes raked wing tips. For it to operate in an all-cargo configuration, additional strengthening of the main deck floor and other areas, including a fixed cargo barrier to the forward area of the aircraft, were also introduced. The main deck cargo door is fitted at the rear of the aircraft and is 12ft 2in (3.71m) wide and 9ft 8in (2.95m) high.

The 777F uses the same engines as its passenger-carrying stablemates, the GE Aerospace GE90-110B. Its noise footprint is below that mandated by the Chapter 4 noise requirement – a useful selling point when so much of its activity takes place during the hours of darkness and close to heavily populated areas.

The 2018 ecoDemonstrator was a collaboration between Boeing and FedEx, which loaned the framer one of its 777 Freighter aircraft. The testing involved 30 new technologies. (Boeing)

Expanding Markets

The growth in the air cargo market has, to a large degree, been a result of the growth of e-commerce, together with the year-round demand for supplies of fresh fruit and vegetables. In addition, those manufacturing companies that use the just-in-time delivery system require reliable jets. The retirement of freighters such as the 767 and DC-10 has also meant that operators have been forced to look for replacements.

Increasing world trade is also fuelling demand for freighter conversions and such is the level of competition within their own markets that package couriers are always looking for lower-cost alternatives to buying new aircraft.

Hold Cargo

Passenger 777s also have an impressive cargo-carrying capacity. For example, the 300 variant has sufficient underfloor space for 50,700lb of cargo. This represents 25% more capacity than even the 747-8I, thus providing useful additional revenue to scheduled airline operators. An example of the volume of the 777-belly hold is that it can easily – and frequently does – accommodate a luxury sports car on a pallet. Not all freight needs to move between major cargo hubs and belly-loaded freight can be carried to destinations which are important, but do not have major cargo-handling facilities, or where there is insufficient requirement for pure freight services.

Deliveries of the 777F began in 2009, customers include the pure-cargo carriers, such as AeroLogic (a Lufthansa/DHL joint venture) and Southern Air. Many airlines have ordered passenger 777s, but also the freighter version – such

as Emirates, Qatar Airways, Air Canada, China Southern Airlines and Korean Air. Four leasing companies: Alatavair, Aerologic, GECAS, and Oak Hill/Avolon have also purchased 777Fs.

Boeing 777-300ER Freighter Conversion

On October 19, 2019, Israel Aerospace Industries (IAI) launched a Boeing 777-300ER freighter conversion option called the 777-300ERSF. Launch customer GE Capital Aviation Services (GECAS) has ordered 15 examples and 15 options.

Although Boeing produces new-build 777 Freighters based on the 777-200LR, IAI said the 777-300ER's greater length means the 777-300ERSF will have 47 standard-sized 96 x 125in (2.4 x 3.2m) pallet positions, ten more than the 777-200LRF.

The conversion involves the addition of a main-deck cargo door, a freighter lining and window plugs to the fuselage, a 9g rigid cargo barrier, deactivation of all

Boeing 777 Freighter N5020K made the type's first flight from Everett-Paine Field on July 14, 2008. (Boeing)

The IAI 777-300ERSF is the first passenger-to-freighter conversion for the Boeing 777.
(Israel Aerospace Industries)

Boeing 777F Characteristics

Wingspan	212ft 7in (64.8m)
Length	209ft 1in (63.7m)
Height	61ft 1in (18.6m)
Max take-off weight	766,800lb (347,815kg)
Max landing weight	575,000lb (260,816kg)
Max zero fuel weight	547,000lb (248,115kg)
Operating empty weight	318,300lb (144,379kg)
Max structural payload	228,700lb (103,737kg)
Total cargo volume	23,051ft³ (652.7m³)
Useable fuel	47,890lb (181,283 lit)
Cruise speed	Mach 0.84
Ceiling	41,000ft (10,100m)
Range	4,970nm (9,200km)
Engines	Two GE Aerospace GE90-110B1/GE90-115B1

Data: Boeing

passenger doors except the first pair, a reinforced fuselage, and an all-new floor structure.

The aircraft has modified environmental control system ducting, provision for powered and non-powered cargo loading, and a main deck temperature control system for the carriage of perishable goods and live animals. There is a crew compartment with up to 11 supernumerary seats, a double bunk crew rest area, and an optional configuration for nine economy class seats.

IAI says the 777-300ERSF offers full commonality with the underfloor cargo configurations and the General Electric GE-115B turbofan engines on the 777-300ER, 777-200LRF and 777-200LR. Rated with 90% spares and 95% ground support equipment commonality with the other aircraft, and no extra simulator training required for flight crew.

The 777-300ERSF is the first Triple Seven aftermarket cargo conversion. It is being marketed as the Big Twin Freighter, a reference to the 'big twin' moniker often

used in relation to the 777-300ER. IAI says the 777-300ERSF has 25% more volume than the 777-200LRF and will burn 21% less fuel per tonne than converted 747-400 freighters.

The 777-300ER is one of the most successful widebody airliners ever, with 850 sold since launch. With older examples leaving their initial operators, there is a ready supply of aircraft for conversion. The 777-300ERSF continues IAI's history of passenger to freighter conversion work on Boeings. It offers conversions for the 737, 747 and 767 and has converted more than 70 jets for GECAS over the last 20 years.

By mid-May 2021, IAI and GE Capital Aviation Services had passed the planned halfway point to obtain a supplemental type certificate for the Boeing 777-300ERSF converted freighter. The first jet to undergo modification by IAI was

N557CC (c/n 32789), which was previously operated Emirates as A6-EBB.

In May 2021, IAI/GECAS described the ongoing work on N557CC as pre-conversion preparation before the physical conversion of the aircraft began on the P2F Line 1 at IAI's Tel Aviv facility. Post conversion and the award of a supplemental type certificate, the 777-300ERSF will be delivered to Kalitta Air.

The prototype aircraft was rolled out at the Tel Aviv facility on January 22, 2023, ahead of its first flight.

Triple Seven Testbed

The Boeing ecoDemonstrator Programme explores new technologies and processes to reduce emissions and noise, improve airlines' efficiency and helps meet environmental and technology innovation goals.

Boeing mechanics began final assembly work on the first 777 Freighter at the company's Everett, Washington, facility in April 2008. The aircraft, F-GUOB (c/n 32965) was delivered to the type's launch customer, Air France, in February 2009. (Boeing)

Qatar Airways received its first Boeing 777 Freighter, registration A7-BFA (c/n 36098) in May 2010. (Boeing)

The project was launched in 2011 and is intended to move ideas through development and into service more quickly by test-flying them. Nine aircraft have been used as testbeds so far. The first was American Airlines' 737-800 N897NN (c/n 33318) in 2012, followed in 2014 by Boeing's own in-house 787-8 Dreamliner N7874 (c/n 40693). Next came 757-233 N757ET (c/n 24627) in 2015 and then Embraer's in-house E170 test aircraft, PP-XJB (c/n 17000003), in 2016. The 2018 phase involved 777 Freighter N878FD (c/n 40684) followed in succession by 777-200 N772ET c/n 29747 (2019), 787-10 N8572C c/n 60768 for Etihad Airways (2020), Alaskan Airlines 737-9 N60436 c/n 19932 (2021), and the current incumbent Surinam Airways 777-200ER N861BC c/n 32336 (2022-2024).

2018 ecoDemonstrator

Each phase of the ecoDemonstrator is a partnership with other organisations from around the industry. Partners involved in the programme to date have included airlines such as American

Airlines and TUI, other original equipment manufacturers like Embraer and Rolls-Royce, systems suppliers such as Rockwell Collins and the public bodies NASA and the Federal Aviation Administration.

The 2018 ecoDemonstrator once again saw Boeing team up with several partners. FedEx supplied the 777F used as the testbed, and other parties involved this time included the Japan Aerospace Exploration Agency (JAXA), Safran and Embraer. In all, 37 technologies were evaluated aboard the Triple Seven spanning propulsion, materials, flight deck enhancements and efficient flight operations.

The 777F involved in the ecoDemonstrator was delivered to FedEx in October 2017, and returned to Boeing in January 2018 for outfitting with the sensors and parts being assessed. It then flew as the ecoDemonstrator for around three months before being stripped of all test equipment and returned to FedEx in June 2018 to resume its normal freighter operations.

Thrust Reverser

One key technology assessed on the ecoDemonstrator 777F was a new, Boeing-designed thrust reverser. Turbofan engine fan sizes are getting larger to provide more thrust, but this means the other engine components such as nacelles, cowlings and thrust reversers are also becoming larger.

For the 2018 ecoDemonstrator Boeing developed a prototype of a new, more compact thrust reverser, which uses some thermoplastic parts to cut weight and works with less hardware to reduce drag while the thruster is not deployed.

Boeing demonstrated the ability to configure the compact thrust reverser to a General Electric GE90 engine [the 777's engine] and test it to make sure it had the same stopping power as a conventional thrust reverser.

The 777F was also fitted with a complete electrical channel supplied by Safran Electrical and Power, encompassing electric power generation and distribution systems, engine and aircraft wiring and electric fans.

Safran designed and developed one of the fastest flight-worthy electrical channels for civil aircraft which is unique in the market and allows future optimisation of the full aircraft electrical system.

According to the company, the system has a single distribution panel managing all functions for control, protection, monitoring and recording of the aircraft's electrical network, and an electrical fan for cooling and cabin ventilation. It claims a variable-frequency geared power generator on the system reduces thermal losses by 60% and saves 15% in weight compared to the existing power-generation system on the 777.

The first Boeing 777F, registration A6-EFH (c/n 35608) was delivered to Dubai Aerospace Enterprise Capital for lease to Emirates SkyCargo in September 2012. (Boeing)

The 777 ecoDemonstrator was responsible for a significant first: it was the first commercial airliner to fly using only alternative fuel. Biofuel demonstrations typically go up to 50% biofuel blended with conventional Jet A-1, but the FedEx 777 flew with 100% biofuel for some of its test flights.

Materials

The 777 ecoDemonstrator carried an additively manufactured tail fin cap with NASA-integrated components. A part in the auxiliary power unit compartment was 3-D printed out of titanium.

Boeing used a part normally milled from a block of titanium with a 10:1 buy-to-fly ratio (the amount of material required to buy the amount of material that flies) and printed the part using additive manufacturing with a 2:1 buy-to-fly ratio, yielding an 80% reduction in the titanium used for the part.

Flight Operations

The ecoDemonstrator programme's efforts to improve environmental performance did not just involve aircraft parts, but also ways of improving the efficiency of flight operations.

The 2018 edition evaluated a synthetic instrument landing system (ILS). Traditional ILS uses a radio beam

Boeing delivered its 50th 777 Freighter to FedEx Express on November 7, 2011. FedEx Express is the largest 777 Freighter operator. (Boeing)

transmitted from the ground, but such systems go down or get blocked by other aircraft. By contrast, a synthetic ILS uses satellite information in the form of GPS signals to create the approach line for the aircraft's systems. The synthetic ILS uses a GPS-based system to position the aircraft like an ILS beam. On the flight deck, the pilot sees the same indications, with the only difference being the indicator using the satellite rather than the ILS beam. The synthetic ILS is not affected by weather, events going on at the airport and allows operators a more consistent way of getting into the airport.

Boeing said the improved accuracy provided by the satellite-based data could enable tighter spacing between aircraft on approach and therefore more efficient operations for both airlines and airports, especially at peak times.

Surfing the Wake

When an aircraft flies, additional lift is created in the air by the vortex it leaves behind it. The 2018 ecoDemonstrator assessed a new prediction algorithm to detect the wake turbulence left by an aircraft flying ahead. This algorithm uses a surveillance function provided by Aviation Communication and Surveillance Systems (ACSS), a joint venture between L3 and Thales.

The tests saw the 777F flown behind another FedEx 777F which demonstrated the ability to predict where the wake is from and then position the aircraft safely and surf the wake to reduce fuel burn. Depending on the aircraft's position on the wave 'surfing' can produce a 5 to 10% improvement in fuel burn. This was the first demonstration of the Boeing-developed algorithm.

Technology improving awareness about the positioning of aircraft in the airways would clearly assist in efficient navigation and route management, so, separate to the wake turbulence work, the ecoDemonstrator 777F was also used to acquire data that will be used to develop the Airborne Collision Avoidance System (ACAS X) standard. This next enhancement of the TCAS II (Traffic Collision and Avoidance System) standard is designed to enhance flight safety, improve navigation aids, and provide efficient route management and fuel optimisation. Another surveillance function supplied by ACSS supported this work.

Boeing and Qatar Airways announced an order for two Boeing 777 Freighters on November 15, 2011, during the Dubai Air Show. It increased the airline's 777 Freighter fleet to eight when delivered. Today the Gulf-based carrier operates a fleet of 27 777 Freighters. (Boeing)

ALL BOEING

An overview of the Luxembourg-based cargo airline, Cargolux.

Cargolux has become a well-established name in the freight market since its inception in March 1970. Europe's biggest all-cargo airline transports freight on both scheduled and charter services between more than 70 destinations in its worldwide network using a fleet of 30 Boeing 747 freighters. It employs 2,500 people, around 1,800 of whom are based in Luxembourg, where the company is headquartered.

The tiny country is an ideal base for freight operations thanks to its central location, with all major European cities accessible by road within 24 hours, and Cargolux collaborates with a team of trucking contractors to move the freight between the airport and its customers.

Cargo Centre

In 1996, Cargolux inaugurated a new cargo centre at its Luxembourg Airport headquarters with a handling capacity of more than a million tonnes per year. Boasting eight aircraft parking spots and more than 110 truck docks for road freight, it included a 920,000ft^2 (85,500m^2) warehouse with stables for live animals, chilled and bonded stores, plus automated equipment for handling the freight. The distance from a truck to an aircraft is just 354ft (108m).

To deal with this expansion, the airport infrastructure was also improved, with the single runway extended to 13,130ft to allow a fully loaded 747 to depart

The 747's future operation is as a high-capacity cargo aircraft. Cargolux uses 14 747-8 Freighters, including LX-VCB (c/n 35806). (Boeing)

to a destination in the Far East. The airport was also certified with a CAT IIIB instrument landing system (ILS) to enable near all-weather operations. Unlike other major northern European airports, Luxembourg is not slot-constrained, thereby making the scheduling of flights far more flexible – although, like other facilities, aircraft movements are not normally allowed between 2200-0500hrs.

The carrier's strongest markets are out of Europe and out of Asia where it has two bases, one in Hong Kong and the other at Zhengzhou, China.

Cargolux became the world's first GDP (Good Distribution Practice) certified airline for the transportation of pharmaceutical products and offers dedicated and qualified carrier and ground handling staff trained in their transportation. The airline's fleet of 747s have four independently controlled temperature zones enabling the transportation of different types of

goods on the same flight with constant temperatures in each zone.

Thanks to the aircraft's nose door, Cargolux has been able to transport a variety of large items, ranging from helicopters to flight simulators, heavy generators, and oil exploration equipment. The airline can carry 84 horses on its 747-400Fs and up to 90 on the 747-8F.

Cargolux Italia

Founded in 2008, Cargolux Italia was established at Milan's Malpensa Airport as a joint venture between Cargolux and various Italian investors as a competitor to Italy's Alitalia Cargo commencing operations in June 2009.

With Milan at the centre of northern Italy's industrial region, it engages in the significant trade of both imported and exported goods. Subsequently, regular destinations from Milan include Hong Kong, Osaka (Japan) and Zhengzhou (China), with occasional services to Africa and the United States.

Currently, Cargolux Italia boasts four Luxembourg-registered Boeing 747-400Fs (registrations LX-SCV, LX-TCV, LX-VCV, LX-YCV) which makes them easily interchangeable with Cargolux's fleet.

Freight Sectors

The airline carries a variety of different cargoes and has eight different 'CV' products in its portfolio, each tailored to the various needs of individual sectors. The different services are all prefixed with the carrier's CV IATA code.

CV Classic looks after general cargo; CV Pharma focuses exclusively on

BOEING 747-8F   LX-VCB

The nose cargo door is one of the 747 Freighter's distinguishing features. (Boeing)

pharmaceutical products; CV Jumbo is a specialist arm with responsibility for outsize cargoes and makes full use of the 747's front-loading cargo doors; and CV Alive is the specialist livestock division. The remaining four specialist sectors are CV Hazmat; CV Precious, which focusses on works of art and precision machinery; CV Power, which concentrates on high value transportation shipments; and CV Fresh – the perishable goods shippers.

Boeing 747-400Fs

The early 1990s were marked by the severe impact on fuel prices caused by the first Gulf War. Undaunted, Cargolux ordered three 747-400F dedicated freighters from Boeing, with an option for three more. The 747-400F offered greater range and was able to fly nonstop from the United States' West Coast to Europe because of the type's fuel efficient General Electric CF6 engines. This larger version of the 747 could also carry around 20 tonnes more than its predecessors, while the fitting of four different air-conditioned zones allowed for perishables and live animals to be carried on the same flight. Other carriers

had placed orders with Boeing for this version, but they were not taken up, making Cargolux the type's debut user.

To make the most of its delivery flight on November 17, 1993, Cargolux's first example, LX-FCV (c/n 25866), flew direct from Seattle to Luxembourg carrying 116 tonnes of cargo. Although the second aircraft, LX-GCV (c/n 25867), joined the fleet just a few weeks later, it was June 1995 before the third aircraft, LX-ICV (c/n 25632), arrived. Cargolux's operational experience with the 747-400 led to further investment in the type and two additional examples, LX-KCV (c/n 25868) and LX-LCV (c/n 25083), joined the fleet in the second half of 1997.

With the carrier enjoying continued growth, it identified a need for even more aircraft and so an order for five Rolls-Royce RB-211-powered 747-400s (along with options for a further two) worth $825m was placed in October 1997. This variant featured opening nose doors, giving the aircraft the ability to carry out-of-gauge cargo up to 20ft in length, such as equipment used for oil drilling and gas exploration.

In 1998, the company's sixth 747-400F, LX-MCV (c/n 29729) was delivered. Cargo

Belgian cartoonist Philippe Cruyt designed a special livery for the 13th Boeing 747-8F delivered to Cargolux (registration LX-VCM c/n 61169), celebrating the carrier's 45th anniversary. (Cargolux)

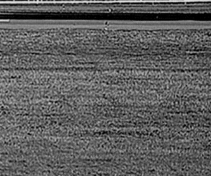

handling processes became digitised, and using the same type across its fleet made the process quicker and easier to implement at home and abroad. As part of the restructuring, the three remaining 747-200Fs were phased out, and another four 747-400s (LX-NCV c/n 29730, LX-OCV c/n 29731, LX-PCV c/n 29732 and LX-RCV c/n 30400) were accepted by the end of 1999, fulfilling the company's ambition to be a one-type operator.

Boeing 747-8

When Cargolux was looking at its fleet renewal options in 2005, it had three aircraft to consider – the Airbus A380 freighter, the Boeing 777F and the Boeing 747-8F.

Cargolux ran the figures and soon dismissed the A380. While it performed well on long sectors it didn't do so well on the shorter flights that make up a lot of Cargolux's network – the carrier's average flight sector is five-and-a-half hours. It also has two decks that would need to be filled and lacks a nose door.

Despite the 777F becoming a popular platform with cargo operators worldwide, Cargolux opted to go for the larger 747-8F. The carrier's business model is based on operating one aircraft type, and with 747-400Fs already in the fleet it had crews available who could be easily trained to operate the new variant. Economics were also good for the 747-8F, particularly on longer routes and with high loads.

Cargolux Boeing 747 Freighters have two cargo holds, one each in the belly and on the main deck. (Key Collection)

Together with Japanese carrier Nippon Cargo Airlines, Cargolux was the launch customer for the Boeing 747-8F, placing an order for ten examples on November 15, 2005. A further four were ordered in March 2007.

The 747-8F is 18.3ft (5.6m) longer than the 747-400F and has a payload capacity of 304,238lb (138 tonnes) – 44,095lb (20 tonnes) more than the older model. Powered by four modern General Electric GEnx-2B turbofan engines each rated at 66,500lbf (296kN), the 747-8 delivers improved fuel efficiency, range, and noise reduction.

The arrival of the 747-8Fs allowed Cargolux to use its 15 747-400Fs more flexibly and they are useful for flying into markets where a smaller capacity aircraft is required. After a series of lengthy delays, Cargolux took delivery of its first 747-8F, LX-VCB (c/n 35806), on October 12, 2011. The 14th and final 747-8F was delivered in September 2016.

MRO Operations

Luxembourg Airport is dominated by Cargolux's large red hangar which opened in May 2009. At 656ft (200m) wide, 295ft (90m) deep and 138ft (42m) high, it can accommodate two Boeing 747-8s or a pair of Airbus A380s. Here Cargolux conducts work up to C checks. The company's

Groundcrew load cargo inside the belly hold
of Boeing 747-8R7F LX-VCC (c/n 35807)
at Luxembourg Airport. (Cargolux)

History

Cargolux was founded on March 4, 1970, as a joint venture between Loftleiðir, Salén, Luxair and private investors. Surplus Loftleiðir Canadair CL-44s were transferred to Cargolux via Salén and the airline flew its first service to Hong Kong in September 1970. In October 1973 Cargolux entered the jet age taking delivery of a Douglas DC-8-61 freighter which was replaced the following spring by a DC-8-55. A total of 13 DC-8s flew for Cargolux and in January 1979 the airline received its first Boeing 747-200F, LX-DCV, with a second example, LX-ECV, following in October 1980. The jumbo has been associated with the company ever since and in 1990 Cargolux placed an order for three 747-400Fs. The first of those aircraft arrived in November 1993 and was the world's first 747-400F in revenue service, carrying 255,736lb (116 tonnes) of cargo on its maiden flight from Seattle, Washington State, to Luxembourg.

aircraft enter the hangar during the early part of the week when demand is lower and are turned around ready to fly again on the Thursday or Friday when the airline is at its busiest.

Cargolux has its own maintenance department to meet the demands of its high daily aircraft utilisation, above 15-16 block hours per day. That utilisation rate can only be achieved if all the departments work together. Maintenance is a core pillar of the company and covers the entire business model.

Workshops behind the hangar conduct repairs on parts, and Cargolux and Atlas Air entered a joint venture holding a common stock of spare parts for the 747-8.

Airlifting outsized cargo is one specialised service offered by Cargolux. One benefit of the Boeing 747-8F is the aircraft's nose cargo door, which eases the loading of long objects. (Cargolux)

Instead of both airlines stocking two spare parts, the joint venture carries four. Two are positioned in Luxembourg and two in Hong Kong to provide flexibility while repairs for the joint venture are conducted at Cargolux's hangar.

Third party maintenance and repair work are also carried out by the company when its schedule permits, and clients include Corsair, Atlas Air, Air Bridge Cargo, and Silk Way.

While specialising in 747 line and hangar-based maintenance, Cargolux also holds approvals for other aircraft, including the 737, 757, 767 and 777. With the fixed costs, personnel, and installation in place, it makes sense for Cargolux to fill the gaps in the maintenance schedule with work for other airlines.

Commercial Co-operation

In December 2013, Cargolux entered into a commercial co-operation agreement with Henan Civil Aviation and Investment Co (HNCA), from that agreement the state of Luxembourg sold the Chinese investor a 35% stake of Cargolux. This resulted in the carrier opening a second hub in Zhengzhou to complement its Luxembourg base as part of its ambition of strong and continuous expansion.

Cargolux has been successful in establishing partnerships with several other airlines, a process that opens new markets for its customers. Such partnerships allow the carrier to serve airports where its aircraft cannot land or where it has no traffic rights. Cargolux airlifts cargo into a major airport where it is transferred onto smaller aircraft operated by the partner airline and distributed around the region. For the partner airlines, the key benefit is access to Cargolux's worldwide network.

A Matter of Choice

Cargolux describes itself as the Global Cargo Carrier of Choice. While the demand for package deliveries is tied

Buying Boeings

In 1978 Cargolux investigated the demand for wide-bodied jets on its services and, following several studies, there were two contenders: the McDonnell Douglas DC-10 or the Boeing 747.

The verdict was in the 747's favour and the inaugural aircraft, a series -200F SCD (side cargo door), was ordered from Boeing in December 1977. This was the first widebody freighter ordered by a European operator and, at the time, was considered a very bold move, not least because its capacity was twice that of the DC-8. In addition, Cargolux began to serve other destinations across Asia and commenced new routes to the United States.

On January 30, 1979, Cargolux took delivery of its first 747F – registration LX-DCV (c/n 20887), christened *City of Luxembourg* – firmly underlining its commitment to become a major all-cargo airline.

The response surrounding the type's larger capacity was positive and immediate, so a second order was placed, with LX-ECV (c/n 21985) delivered in October the following year. The CV in the jet's registration was a nod to the International Air Transport Association's prefix for the airline.

Cargolux's growth exceeded even the most optimistic expectations, but like any business it was invariably a roller-coaster ride. During the early 1980s, the global economy took a significant downturn, with a consequent increase in interest rates. With the demand for air cargo decreasing, revenues were severely affected. Cargolux laid off a third of its workforce and began negotiations to restructure. Reaching a deal with several Luxembourg-based banks, these superseded Loftleiðir and Salén's shares. With the increasing use of digital equipment, Cargolux also devised a system called Cargo Handling and Management Planning (CHAMP), which integrated its entire operation and introduced greater efficiency and cost savings.

Apart from Aero Uruguay, Cargolux had operated without any co-operation agreements, but as the passenger airlines began to form calculated partnerships it was logical for cargo carriers to follow suit. China was beginning to open-up to the West, so a strategic alliance was agreed with China Airlines in 1982. However, its key routes were still those to the Far East and the United States, typically operated by the 747. By then, the company's remaining DC-8s were primarily being used to cover ad-hoc charters and often offered to other operators on short-term leases.

To aid its recovery, it re-entered the Hajj market with a passenger-configured 747 leased from Boeing, which continued for several years. With the 747s then firmly established in its fleet, Cargolux withdrew its DC-8s and, by the end of 1985, had sold them to other operators. By then, the business world had largely recovered from the economic downturn and three more 747-200s were delivered in 1986.

Aircraft Names

Each Cargolux Boeing 747 freighter is named after a city in the Grand-Duchy of Luxembourg where the airline is headquartered. The only exception is LX-VCJ which is named *City of Zhengzhou* in recognition of the airline's second hub in China.

Boeing 747-400Fs
LX-ECV c/n 37303 *City of Grevenmacher*
The city of Grevenmacher is located near the German border and situated on the left bank of the Moselle River in a wine growing region. The town is one site of the six regional headquarters of the Grand Ducal Police

LX-GCL c/n 34150 *City of Sandweiler*
Sandweiler is situated in the south of the country and home to Luxembourg Findel airport. It is home to a German war cemetery with 10,913 graves of soldiers that fell in the Luxemburgish-Belgian and Luxemburgish-German border areas during World War Two.

LX-ICL c/n 30805 *City of Mersch*
Mersch is in the centre of Luxembourg. The town offers a variety of attractions related to culture, nature, and tourism. It is a place full of history with examples of inherited medieval architecture like Schönfels and Pettingen castles.

LX-JCV c/n 35171 No name

LX-KCL c/n 35326 *City of Junglinster*
Junglister is situated in the heart of the Grand-Duchy. With just over 2,000 inhabitants, the town is a hotspot for hot air balloon flights over Luxembourg.

LX-LCL c/n 35234 *City of Clervaux*
The city of Clervaux is in the northern part of Luxembourg close to the areas where the Battle of Clervaux and the Battle of the Bulge were fought in 1944. This town hosts one of the most famous and longest running photography exhibitions, Edward Steichen's 'The Family of Man' which was added to UNESCO's Memory of the World Register.

LX-MCL c/n 35232 *City of Bourscheid*
Bourscheid is in the northeastern part of Luxembourg. Bourscheid Castle is one of the largest and most important medieval castles between the Meuse and the Rhine.

LX-NCL c/n 35170 *City of Ettelbrück*
The city of Ettelbrück is situated in the heart of the Grand Duchy and is the biggest town in the north of the country. The local Christmas market is the oldest in Luxembourg and the agricultural fair attracts over 30,000 visitors every year.

LX-OCV c/n 29731 *City of Niederanven*
Niederanven is situated in the south of the country. Part of the Luxembourg-Findel International Airport is located within the city. It is a founding member of the Douzelage, a unique twinning association of 24 towns across the European Union.

LX-RCV c/n 30400 *City of Walferdange*
The city of Walferdange is in the centre of Luxembourg, in the Alzette valley. Until 2015 parts of the University of Luxembourg were based in the town. In former times gypsum mines were an important industrial sector for Walferdange.

LX-SCV c/n 29733 *Tre Cime Di Lavaredo*
The Tre Cime di Lavaredo are three battlement-like peaks in the Sexten Dolomites of northeastern Italy. The summits are one of the most famous mountain groups in the Alps and part of the linguistic boundary between German-speaking and Italian-speaking majorities.

LX-TCV c/n 30401 *Monte Cervino* (Matterhorn)
Monte Cervino is a 4,478m high mountain in the Alps, straddling the main watershed and border between Switzerland and Italy. It is a near-symmetrical pyramidal peak, making it one of the highest summits in the Alps and Europe.

Boeing 747-400Fs Operated by Cargolux Italia

LX-UCV c/n 33827 *City of Bertrange*
The city of Bertrange in southwestern Luxembourg is home to the National Research Center for Archeology and the Schauwenburg Castle which dates back to the Middle Ages.

LX-VCV c/n 34235 *Monviso*
The Monviso is 3,841m high and situated in Italy close to the French border, is the highest mountain of the Cottian Alps, and well known for its pyramid-like shape standing taller than all its neighbouring peaks.

LX-WCV c/n 35804 *City of Pétange*
Pétange is situated in southwestern Luxembourg and lies on the borders with both Belgium and France. The town is influenced by the steel industry and nowadays a lot of manufacturing companies are located there.

LX-YCV c/n 34235 *Monte Rosa*
The Monte Rosa is a 4.634m high ice-covered mountain massif located in the eastern part of the Pennine Alps, between Switzerland and Italy. It is the highest mountain of Switzerland and the second highest mountain of the Alps and Western Europe.

Boeing 747-8Fs
LX-VCA c/n 35808 *City of Vianden*
Vianden is situated in the northwest of the country near to the German border. Due to the Vianden castle and its location in the Our valley Vianden is one of the most popular tourist towns in Luxembourg.

LX-VCB c/n 35806 *City of Esch-Sur-Alzette*
Esch-sur-Alzette is the second biggest city in Luxembourg with a population of more than 33,280. The former industrial city is home to many cultural institutions and the new location of the University of Luxembourg.

LX-VCC c/n 35807 *Spirit of Cargolux*
To celebrate its jubilee in 2020, LX-VCC was re-branded with a special 50-year logo reflecting its long-standing history. The aircraft also bears the name *Spirit of Cargolux*, to honour employees who have contributed to the airline's success throughout the years.

LX-VCD c/n 35809 *City of Luxembourg*
The city of Luxembourg is the capital of the Grand Duchy and the country's biggest city. The capital is the seat of several institutions of the European Union, including the European ●●●

●●● Court of Justice, and an important financial centre. The old town and the ancient quarters are part of the UNESCO Cultural World Heritage.

LX-VCE c/n 35810 *City of Echternach*
Echternach is in the east of the country near the German border and is the oldest town in Luxembourg. It is well known for the Echternach dancing procession, which is part of UNESCO Cultural World Heritage.

LX-VCF c/n 35811 *Facemask*
LX-VCF, nicknamed *Facemask*, features a surgical mask design on the nose-cargo door along with the Luxembourg government's slogan "Not without my mask", a testimony to Cargolux's on-going engagement in the fight against the global pandemic.

LX-VCG c/n 35812 *City of Diekirch*
The city of Diekirch is situated in the northeast of Luxembourg on the banks of the Sauer River. The main barracks of the Luxembourg army are situated in the city as is a brewery carrying the city's name.

LX-VCH c/n 35821 *City of Dudelange*
Dudelange is the third biggest city in Luxembourg and is situated near the French border. The town is one of the most important industrial locations of the country and was the former production site of the steel group ARBED.

LX-VCI c/n 35822 *City of Troisvierges*
The city of Troisvierges is the northernmost commune of Luxembourg. The town is the site of the start of hostilities on the Western Front in World War One.

LX-VCJ c/n 38077 *City of Zhengzhou*
Zhengzhou lies on the southern bank of the Yellow River and is the provincial capital of Henan Province in east-central China. As a prefecture-level city, it serves as the political, economic, technological, and educational centre of the province, and a major transportation hub for central China.

LX-VCK c/n 38078 *City of Contern*
Contern has a rich culture full of well-known traditions like the Festival de la Bande dessinée, a cartoon festival. The name of the town has Celtic origins, and the history goes back to pre-Roman times.

LX-VCL c/n 35823 *Joe Sutter-Father of the Boeing 747*
Joe Sutter is a former engineer for the Boeing Airplane Company and manager of the design team for the Boeing 747 aircraft. Due to his great work, he was later called the father of the Boeing 747.

LX-VCM c/n 61169 *City of Rédange-Sur-Attert*
Rédange-sur-Attert is in the west of the Grand Duchy, near the border with Belgium, on the Attert River, a tributary of the Alzette.

LX-VCN c/n 38076 *Spirit of Schengen*
Schengen is a small village in far southeastern Luxembourg, near the tripoint where the borders of Germany, France and Luxembourg meet. The Schengen Agreement, a treaty which led to the creation of Europe's borderless Schengen Area, was signed in this town. The international convention allowed opening of the borders and thus the free circulation of inhabitants.

---

inextricably to the need for air cargo, every carrier must try to stay one step ahead of the competition.

In meeting that goal, Cargolux finalised an order of 10 777-8 Freighters with options for six additional airplanes, with a signing ceremony at Cargolux's Luxembourg HQ on October 12, 2022. Selection of the 777-8F was announced at the 2022 Farnborough International Airshow as Cargolux's preferred choice as the replacement for its 747-400 Freighter fleet.

The decision underlined Cargolux's commitment to establishing long-term sustainability. Launched in January 2022, the 777-8F offers near-identical payload and range capabilities as the 747-400F, 30% better fuel efficiency and emissions, 25% better operating costs per tonne, and a noise footprint up to 60% smaller than its predecessors.

Further to the 777-8F order, on January 19, 2023, Cargolux announced it had entered into a long-term support agreement with GE Aerospace for the GE9X engine: the powerplant of its nascent Boeing 777-8Fs. The GE9X is the most powerful aircraft engine yet built, the quietest GE Aerospace engine ever produced based on pounds of thrust per decibel, and offers up to 15% better fuel efficiency, and the lowest NOx emissions in its class.

The agreement also includes a multi-year GE TrueChoice service agreement and an order for two spare engines. TrueChoice incorporates an array of GE capabilities and customisations across an engine's lifecycle underpinned by GE data and analytic capabilities to help reduce maintenance burden and service disruptions for customers.

Each of the company's aircraft are named after Luxembourgish towns and cities (see panel). Boeing 747-8F LX-VCV (c/n 34825) is named after the commune of Walferdange, just north of Luxembourg city. (Key Collection)

Cargo Choreography

Martyn Cartledge and Spencer Bennett report on the nightly choreography of cargo and freighters at East Midlands Airport.

East Midlands Airport has accessibility on its side; the cities of Nottingham, Derby, and Leicester are all within a 20-mile radius and, as it sits directly next to the M1 Motorway, it is linked to an excellent onward road network. This puts it within a four-hour truck journey of 90% of the population of England and Wales.

In addition, there is the new East Midlands Gateway nearby, which incorporates a 50-acre Strategic Rail Freight Interchange (SRFI).

Most cargo is moved during the night. The numbers of cargo movements vary throughout the week ranging from 50 arrivals and departures during a night, while on the peak days of Tuesday, Wednesday, and Thursday it often reaches up to 80 daily movements and occasionally even 90. Friday to Monday is rather less busy and numbers fluctuate throughout the week depending on the demand at any given time.

East Midlands Airport (owned by the Manchester Airports Group or MAG) is a major hub for both UPS and DHL having extensive facilities in addition to large operations by the Royal Mail and FedEx. Amazon also has a site nearby. These organisations have invested hundreds of millions of pounds into their bespoke handling facilities at the airport in the last two years. In total East Midlands has five airside cargo terminals offering more than 650,000ft^2 of undercover cargo handling area, an EU-approved border post for inspections of animal produce, plus more than two million sq. ft of dedicated cargo apron space for loading and unloading of freighter aircraft. It's a vast operation.

The authors caught up with some of the key players at the airport to find out more about the scale and importance of freight operations.

Growth

Stephen Harvey, MAG's head of cargo explained: "The EMA cargo operation sees just over 1,000 tonnes of goods pass through the airport each day, equating to over one million items."

These goods are split approximately 50/50 between inbound and outbound with an annual value of £11bn.

The airport has approximately 30 cargo stands in use each night, which are shared between four operators, as Steve elaborated: "At the busiest times there could be 18-20 aircraft on the ground at any one time."

DHL Express is the largest operator at the airport with its own dedicated ground control centre and an 1,883,684ft^2

facility. The associated apron and stands are all owned by MAG but in practice, the 18 stands are rarely, if ever, used by any airline not operating for DHL. Peter Bardens, vice president of UK Hubs, DHL Express said: "On average, we have 23 flights on a weeknight. We've seen huge growth in volumes coming from e-commerce. This area has been growing in recent years but now it's been massively accelerated, and we don't expect it to end anytime soon. The reach of the airline is truly global with EMA acting as a hub between the US and Europe. Our busiest routes are to Leipzig, Brussels, and various destinations in the United States."

Airlines using this facility are mainly DHL Air UK and European Air Transport with Airbus A300s, A330s and Boeing 757s and 767s. There are many other airlines, however, that fly for the company. Some are in the DHL livery; others wear their own, or some form of combination of the two. The airlines include AeroLogic Boeing 777s that arrive from the Leipzig hub as part of a joint venture between

DHL Express and Lufthansa Cargo. Canada's Cargojet operates from one of the major DHL destinations, Cincinnati, using a Boeing 767. ABX Air also flies 767 services from Cincinnati in addition to Chicago. Kalitta Air uses a 747 on services connecting EMA with Leipzig, Brussels, Cincinnati, and Los Angeles.

Boeing 737s are possibly the most prolific freighter type at EMA. West Atlantic Cargo Airlines, ASL Airlines Hungary, ASL Airlines Ireland and Cargo Air of Bulgaria all use the type on their DHL services from around Europe, as well as for other companies at the airport. BlueBird Nordic regularly flies in a Boeing 737-400 full of fish from Keflavík, Iceland.

At the other end of the scale, Swiftair operates an ATR 42 on a service for West Atlantic from Guernsey, while the RVL group flies possibly the smallest aircraft,

a Reims Cessna F406 Caravan II from the Isle of Man and Dublin.

The impact of the COVID-19 pandemic not only meant greater volumes for DHL in 2020, but also new services. Amerijet now operates a 767 from Cincinnati and back out to New York-JFK. There is now also a once-weekly service by AirBridgeCargo Airlines utilising 747s including its new 747-8F variant from Hong Kong, as Peter Bardens explained: "In early 2021, we launched the UK's first direct cargo route from Asia, with the first flight landing at East Midlands Airport. The route was introduced in response to the increasing demand from businesses for shipments from Asia, across the spectrum of medical, industrial and consumer goods. Our EMA hub is a facilitator of international trade, something that this new route made a significant contribution to."

The DHL apron at East Midlands Airport with three A300-600Fs, a single Boeing 757F, and a Boeing 777F.
(Martyn Cartledge)

Cargo containers are offloaded from Boeing 767-300F, N311UP (c/n 27741) operated by UPS. (Martyn Cartledge)

MNG Airlines is another addition, operating an Airbus A300-600F from Istanbul and onwards to Luton.

Other Operators

UPS is next in terms of tonnage and now operates from a brand-new purpose-built building. UPS uses the Boeing 767 for most of its services either with its own aircraft or those of Star Air. The UPS examples only operate from/to Philadelphia and Cologne, while Star Air also flies to Cologne as well as domestically to Edinburgh and Belfast.

It is believed that UPS would prefer to increase the size of aircraft on many of its services, but operational logistics means that this is not possible. The chances of ever seeing an MD-11 or 747 in UPS livery at EMA are therefore somewhat remote.

Royal Mail has a 350,000ft^2 distribution warehouse, with West Atlantic 737s making full use of it alongside ATR 72s and Saab 340s of Loganair.

FedEx/TNT is the smallest operation, using their own Boeing 757s and aircraft from ASL Airlines Belgium on services to Liège.

FedEx increased its market share in 2016 with the acquisition of rival TNT, although the purchase excluded the TNT airline arm which was subsequently sold to ASL Airlines which continues to run flights for FedEx into EMA. Its presence is quite extensive with aircraft operated via its different arms (ASL Airlines Hungary, ASL Airlines Ireland, ASL Airlines France and ASL Airlines Belgium), with types ranging from the ATR 72 to Boeing 737 and 757. In addition to DHL and FedEx/TNT, ASL Airlines also operates for Amazon which has a new one million sq. ft facility in the nearby East Midlands Gateway.

Amazon handles some of its own freight as well as using the other companies on site. Other than ASL Airlines France and Ireland, Amazon uses CargoLogic Germany, Titan Airways and DHL for its consignments.

Security enhancements are also a consideration – they are not only seen in passenger terminals. Freight must be screened for illicit and undeclared dangerous items, but with an extra emphasis on radiological and nuclear materials. At each end of the apron there is an innocuous-looking device, which forms part of Project Cyclamen.

This programme was initiated to manage the risk of non-conventional terrorism in the United Kingdom following Al-Qaeda's attacks against the United States in 2001.

Any shipments from outside the UK must be driven through these portals, which would trigger an alarm to Border Force staff should anything radiological be detected.

In practice, these devices do not create any delays, as the freight simply passes through without needing unpacking.

German cargo airline AeroLogic operates into EMA on behalf of DHL utilising Boeing 777Fs. (Martyn Cartledge)

One of the daily cargo airlines using EMA in support of DHL is European Air Transport which flies A300-600Fs. (Martyn Cartledge)

Pandemic Boost

The COVID-19 effect was significant for EMA and its operators. With passenger services suffering, cargo operations at East Midlands saw a considerable increase, as Stephen Harvey explained: "Over the summer months, traditionally the quieter time of year for air cargo, volumes at EMA were significantly up." The busiest period of the year is that leading up to Christmas. In November 2020, the airport handled 41,613 tonnes of cargo, up 26.4% from the 2019 figure of 32,925 tonnes. December 2020 was a record month for EMA with 46,320 tonnes passing through, a massive 43% increase on the previous year's total of 32,251 tonnes.

Peter Bardens expanded on this saying: "Continuing to trade globally was an important factor in providing stability to global economies in this period, whether it was importing vital products like PPE at the height of the crisis, to supporting businesses to sell online to other markets.

"Throughout the earlier stages of the pandemic, we had to adapt quickly to ensure our operations could support the growth in demand and shifting patterns in aviation. For example, we would usually use passenger airlines to transport products around the world, but as these flights reduced, we had to rely more on our network aircraft."

This increase was driven by changes in consumer habits which, already undergoing a transformation, were exacerbated by more people being at home due to the pandemic. According to the Office of National Statistics, this caused the percentage of UK shopping conducted online to rise from 19% in February 2020 to 36% in November.

Aboudy Nasser, group aviation director for MAG, explained: "While much was made of the changes to the way people travel, behind the scenes our airports have been leading the charge in helping the logistics sector adapt to rising demand for dedicated air cargo and changes in the way goods are transported." When pandemic lockdowns began, in early March 2020, EMA suffered like other airports with passenger flights reduced drastically while there was increased demand for cargo leading to an increase in the number of flights for the latter.

Seizing the Moment

It's not surprising that the pandemic sat at the top of the list of obstacles faced by airports, but it also presented some opportunities. Stephen Harvey acknowledged the fact that not all businesses faced the same stresses: "EMA's cargo operation was in stark contrast to the collapse in passenger traffic faced by the UK's aviation sector." This was underpinned by the rise in tonnage. Peter Bardens added that the airport's 'bread and butter' is e-commerce and B2C [business to customer] items of the integrator-led express freight market.

The airport oversees a wide range of cargo, and these have included Formula 1 cars, aero engines from Rolls-Royce in nearby Derby, valuable works of art, satellites, and stone-crushing equipment.

Peter Bardens detailed further interesting cargoes: "Among the quirkier shipments, and always a favourite, are the animals we have repatriated through the hub including gorillas and tigers. We were proud to be able to support the response to the COVID-19 pandemic through our involvement in the Masks For NHS Heroes campaign."

Operating in DHL colours, European Air Transport Leipzig has two A330-200Fs in its fleet. (Martyn Cartledge)

Boeing 767Fs operated by Amerijet are regular visitors to EMA from the DHL hub at Cincinnati. (Martyn Cartledge)

Freighters parked in front of DHL's warehouse building next to the western ramp at EMA. (Martyn Cartledge)

M-Dee Eleven

Designed with a three-engine configuration, the McDonnell Douglas MD-11 is distinctive and visually striking. Less successful as a passenger aircraft, the MD-11 continues to earn its keep as a freighter.

The first MD-11 freighter built, N601FE (c/n 48401), was delivered to FedEx Express on June 27, 1991. (FedEx)

Originally designed and built by the McDonnell Douglas Aircraft Company at its Long Beach, California facility and based on the DC-10, the MD-11 widebody trijet was produced in passenger and freighter variants. By comparison to the DC-10, the MD-11 features a longer fuselage, an increased wingspan with winglets, refined air foils on the wing and tailplane, new engines, and a greater use of composite material.

Equipped with an advanced common flightdeck, the cockpit features six interchangeable CRT displays, an electronic instrument system, a dual flight management system, a central fault display system, and Category IIIB auto-landing capability for bad-weather operations.

The MD-11 also features a computer-assisted pitch stability augmentation system with a fuel ballast tank in the tailplane, and part computer-driven horizontal stabiliser, and hydraulic fuses to prevent catastrophic loss of control in the event of hydraulic failure.

MD-11F N529FE (c/n 48624) was the first jet to be retired from FedEx service in 2023. The aircraft was flown to Southern California Airport at Victorville on January 3, 2023. (FedEx)

Given its high landing speed and the need for precise control, the MD-11 is known for being difficult to land. To counter this, McDonnell-Douglas and subsequently Boeing redesigned flight deck features and the flight control software in a bid to make the aircraft safer and easier to fly.

The MD-11F freighter features:
- A forward port-side cargo door measuring 140 x 102in (3.6 × 2.6m) which uses an independent hydraulic system with pressure supplied by an electrically driven pump. If electrical power is not available, the cargo door can be operated by a manual hydraulic pump.

McDonnell-Douglas MD-11 Variants

Designation	Variant	Launch date	Production run	Total built
MD-11 First variant	Passenger variant	1986	1988-1998	131
MD-11F Second variant	Freighter	1986	1988-2000	53
MD-11C Third variant	Combi featured a cargo door aft of the wings	1986	1991-1992	
MD-11CF	Convertible freighter	1991-1992		
MD-11ER		1994		

- MD-11 freighters were ordered by major operators FedEx, China Eastern, Lufthansa Cargo, Martinair, EVA, and Saudi Arabian Airlines.
- All five MD-11C aircraft were built for Alitalia.
- Amsterdam-based Martinair was the launch customer for the MD-11CF convertible freighter.
- The last of 200 production-series MD-11 aircraft was built in October 2000.
- P2F conversions were completed via a McDonnell-Douglas engineered programme by Aeronavali and subsequently ST Aero.

ABOVE: Delivered to FedEx Express in October 1992, N607FE (c/n 48547) was placed in temporary storage between February and November 2020. (FedEx)

BELOW: MD-11F N586FE (c/n 48487) was converted to freighter configuration in the mid-1990s. Originally configured as a passenger aircraft, the jet operated with American Airlines. (FedEx)

- A main-deck volume of 15,530ft^3 (440m^3).
- Max payload of 200,151lb (90,787kg).
- The capacity to transport 26 pallets, either 88 x 125in (2.2 x 3.2m) or 96 x 125in (2.4 x 3.2m) type.
- The lower deck compartment features doorway omni-directional rollers; a doorway self-retracting lateral/longitudinal powered roller; a centreline conveyor roller, side guide rails; centreline lateral restraint latch; and tie-down points for bulk cargo.
- Winglets reportedly improve fuel efficiency by about 2.5%.
- A smaller empennage than the DC-10.

MD-11 Launch

McDonnell Douglas launched the MD-11 on December 30, 1986, with an order book containing 52 firm orders and options for 40 more from ten airlines and two leasing companies. The pre-New Year launch was not for one variant but three: passenger, combi, and freighter. Created from a plan for a stretched DC-10 variant, the company's earlier-model trijet which had a tarnished reputation following some high-profile accidents, McDonnell Douglas designated the new aircraft as the MD-11.

The framer started the assembly process of the first MD-11 prototype on March 9, 1988. Less than two years later, on January 10, 1990, the prototype undertook the type's maiden flight from Long Beach. Following

a ten-month flight test programme, the Federal Aviation Administration awarded the type certification on November 8, 1990. Helsinki-based carrier Finnair took delivery of the first production-series aircraft on December 7, 1990, which entered revenue-earning service on December 20. The first two production-series MD-11 freighters were delivered to FedEx in the spring of 1991.

MD-11F Characteristics	
Length	GE-powered aircraft 202ft 2in/61.60m Pratt & Whitney-powered 200ft 11in/61.20m
Width	19ft 9in (6.0m) fuselage 225in (5.72m) cabin
Wingspan	170ft 6in (51.97m) span, 3,648ft² (338.9m²) area
Height	57ft 11in (17.65m)
Max take-off weight	602,500lb (273,294kg) ER 630,500lb (285,988kg)
Operating empty weight	248,567lb (112,748kg)
Max payload	202,733lb (91,962kg)
Fuel capacity	38,615 US gal (146,173 lit) 258,721lb (117,356kg)
Engines	Three Pratt & Whitney PW4460 high-bypass turbofan engines. Or three Pratt & Whitney PW4462 high-bypass turbofan engines each rated at 62,000lbf (280kN). Or Three General Electric CF6-80C2D1F high-bypass turbofan engines each rated at 61,500lbf (274kN). Two engines are mounted on wing pylons and one in the vertical tail.
Speed	Mach 0.83 – Mach 0.88
Range	3,592nm (6,652km)
Ceiling	43,000ft (13,100m)
Main deck	26 96×125in pallets or 34 88×108in pallets
Main deck volume	21,530ft² (609.7m³)
Lower deck	32 LD3s

Retirements

After 23 years of service, Lufthansa Cargo operated its last MD-11F flight on October 17, 2021. MD-11F D-ALCC (c/n 48783) landed at Frankfurt from New York-JFK shortly after 12 noon, the last of the type registered in Europe. In October D-ALCC, the last of 19 MD-11Fs operated by Lufthansa Cargo, was transferred to Western Global Airways registered as N783SN. The carrier has replaced the MD-11F with Boeing 777Fs.

United Parcel Service Airlines is also retiring its fleet of 40 MD-11Fs. Aircraft c/n 48634 departed Louisville International Airport bound for Southern California Airport at Victorville on January 2. The carrier plans to retire a further five MD-11Fs during 2023. UPS MD-11Fs are being replaced with Boeing 767-300 freighters, 80 of which are already in service with another 27 on order.

Another major MD-11F operator, FedEx Express which operates a fleet of 54 aircraft has announced its plan to start the phase-out this year. FedEx MD-11s are being replaced with Boeing 767-300 and Boeing 777 freighters: 27 767Fs and eight 777Fs are on order, increasing its current fleet of 125 767Fs and 53 777Fs.

Originally operated on lease by Garuda followed by Varig, N575FE (c/n 48500) was converted to freighter configuration in 2005-2006. (FedEx)

TWENTY-EIGHT FOXTROTS

An overview of the Boeing 747-8F in service with cargo carrier UPS which operates more of the type than any other airline.

The introduction of the 747-8F to UPS Airlines service in the autumn of 2017 and the carrier's two orders both attest to the state of the air cargo market. When the airline announced the second 747-8F order, they emphasised the jumbos would add additional capacity to their network rather than replace older high-capacity 747-400Fs and MD-11Fs already in its fleet.

Large Capacity

The 747-8F has 4,245ft³ (120m³) more cargo volume than the preceding 747-400F, of which UPS Airlines operates 12.

A 747-8F has 34 main-deck pallet positions and 12 lower-deck positions and a maximum cargo payload of 307,600lb (139,525kg), compared to a 747-400F's 30 main-deck and nine lower-deck positions and 258,600lb (117,298kg) payload, according to UPS Airlines figures.

Captain Doug Lainey, the UPS Airlines 747-8 implementation manager said: "It's about 16% more volume and then about 19% more payload. On a Hong

The 747-8F is being used by UPS Airlines on its key trunk routes from its Louisville base to Asia and the Middle East. (Boeing)

UPS Airlines operates a fleet of 28 Boeing 747-8 Freighters. (Boeing)

Kong–Louisville flight, where a 747-400F would carry maybe 250,000lb of payload, we're looking at close to 300,000lb."

The 747-8F's larger size from the 747-400F provides the extra capacity. Both 747-8 variants (the 747-8 Intercontinental passenger version and the 747-8F) are 250ft 2in (76.3m) long compared to the 231ft 8in-long (70.7m) 747-400, thanks to a 160in (4.1m) fuselage stretch fore of the wing and a 60in (1.6m) stretch aft of the wing. The 747-8's wingspan is 224ft 5in (68.4m), compared to the 747-400's 212ft (64.9m). Height is virtually identical: 63ft 6in (19.35m) compared to 63ft 8in (19.40m).

Impact on the Network

Given the 747-8F's capacity it was inevitable that UPS Airlines would place its big new freighter into service on routes between its Worldport hub at Louisville, Kentucky and the Middle East, Asia and the company's European hub at Cologne, Germany, some of the key long-haul trunk routes on its network where the need for capacity is greatest.

The 747-8F's combination of capacity and 4,200nm (7,778km) range is influencing how the carrier is connecting Worldport with other key air cargo centres worldwide. Most notably, the airline operates a round-the-world route linking North America, the Middle East, and Asia.

Captain Laney explained: "Originally, we had a 747-400F that flew

Boeing 747-8 Freighter Characteristics	
Length	250ft 2in (76.3m)
Wingspan	224ft 5in (68.4m)
Height	63ft 6in (19.4m)
Max taxi weight	990,000lb (449,061kg)
Max take-off weight	987,000lb (447,700kg)
Max zero fuel weight	727,000lb (329,795kg)
Max landing weight	763,000lb (346,095kg)
Operating empty weight	485,300lb (220,130kg)
Max cargo payload	307,600lb (139,525kg)
Max structural payload	292,400lb (132,630kg)
Useable fuel	59,734 US gal (226,118 lit)
Total cargo volume	30,288ft³ (857m³)
Main-deck volume capacity	24,462ft³ (692.7m³) consisting of 34 pallets
Lower-hold volume capacity	5,826ft³ (165m³) consisting of 12 pallets, 2 LD1 containers and bulk storage of 496ft³ (14.0m³)
Cargo positions	34 main deck, 12 lower deck
Max speed	Mach 0.85
Range	4,200nm (7,778km)
Engines	Four GE Aerospace GEnx GE-2B67 engines, each generating 66,500lb (296kN) of maximum take-off thrust
Sources: Boeing, General Electric, UPS Airlines	

General Electric GEnx-2B engines and a new wing are key differences between the 747-8 and its 747-400 predecessor. (Boeing)

Shenzhen–Anchorage–Louisville. Because of the stage length a 747-8F can fly and the payload it can carry, instead of running out to Anchorage we can go the other way and answer the need for Middle East volume and go [from Louisville] to Dubai, then from Dubai to Shenzhen and then from Shenzhen to Anchorage and back to Louisville."

UPS says it has taken a day off the transit time for cargo between Louisville and Asia. At 6,691nm (12,392km), the route is the furthest scheduled service ever operated by the carrier and reflects UPS' intentions to expand its presence in Dubai.

Captain Lainey explained how the 747-8F's arrival has had other impacts on UPS Airlines. The carrier has been able to release 747-400Fs from some trunk routes and instead put these aircraft on sectors traditionally served by MD-11Fs. This has increased volume capacity on some flights. For example, the airline says putting 747-400Fs on its Cologne–Dubai flight better serves customers in Europe connecting to the Indian subcontinent, the Middle East, and Africa. According to the airline, UPS MD-11Fs have 207,129lb (93,952kg) payload capacity compared to a 747-400F's 258,600lb (117,299kg).

In turn, moving the 747-400Fs has freed up some MD-11Fs to provide additional lift on US services, which itself has enabled Airbus A300Fs, Boeing 757Fs and Boeing 767Fs on these routes to be flexibly moved around the network as market demands dictate.

Differences and Commonality

Beyond the larger size, there are several differences between the 747-8F and its 747-400F forebear. The 'Dash Eight' has new General Electric GEnx GE-2B67 engines, which according to GE's figures provide 66,500lb (296kN) of maximum take-off thrust compared to the 56,400-63,300lb (251-282kN) generated by the GE CF6, Pratt & Whitney PW4000 and Rolls-Royce RB211 engine choices on the 747-400F. The UPS 747-400Fs have CF6 engines.

The 747-8F has a new wing featuring raked tips, fly-by-wire spoilers, and outboard ailerons to save weight and cut drag. Double-slotted inboard and single-slotted outboard flaps, an aileron droop and redesigned flap track fairings are designed to optimise low-speed performance and cut noise, with Krueger flaps designed to assist in low-speed handling.

With these key airframe and engine differences, maximising commonality with the 747-400 in other areas was a prime goal for Boeing. Other than a larger tow bar, the servicing requirements needed for the 747-8F such as pneumatic start carts, ground power units, portable loaders and trucks supplying electrical power, conditioned air, and water, are the same as those for the 747-400F.

Cargo handling equipment used on the ramp, including the hydraulic lift used to load containers and pallets, and the aircraft's internal power drive system powering the rollers that move payloads into position on the main and lower decks are also identical to the 747-400F.

Commonality minimises change to the spares inventory, which translates to lower costs. Captain Lainey said: "There's about 30% commonality in total with the 747-400F. That probably doesn't sound like a lot, but that is a significant number when you look at the total number of parts required for the inventory."

The 747-8 has the same type rating as the 747-400, even though the flight deck has technologies brought across from the 787 Dreamliner, such as multifunction displays, Boeing Class 3 electronic flight bag provision, an electronic checklist, an airport moving map display, integrated approach navigation, GPS autoland, a vertical situation display and an onboard network server.

Captain Lainey said the flight deck is "a blend of the old with some of the new," which has minimised training requirements. He explained: "747-400F-qualified pilots go through a 747-8F differences training course. Essentially, this is one day of computer-based training about systems and two days in what we call an IPT, an integrated procedures trainer, and what other people call a flat panel trainer or a crew-based simulator. After that, they are signed-off to go and fly; there's no aircraft training or check ride required.

The UPS corporate livery and World Services title are recognised all over the world on packages to Boeing 747s. (Boeing)

"Boeing engineers and flight test folks did a great job in making it fly as closely as possible to the 747-400 to minimise differences. It's a pleasure to fly; as big as it is, it does not feel big and has nice, soft controls. Boeing designed it so the transition is as easy as possible for the flight crews, [who] absolutely love the aircraft."

Boeing says the 747-8F burns 16% less fuel, produces 16% lower carbon dioxide emissions compared to the 747-400F and operates at 52% below International Civil Aviation Organization Committee on Aviation Environmental Protection 6 limits for nitrous oxide emissions.

According to Captain Lainey, Boeing is "hitting or exceeding" the performance targets to which it committed when it sold the 747-8F to UPS Airlines. He praised the jet's "pretty stunning" quiet performance; Boeing cites a 30% smaller noise footprint compared to a 747-400. He added: "The despatch reliability is very high. Normally you get a few problems, but, in this case, we're seeing very high reliability even a year into the programme. It's exceeded my expectations. I knew it was a great aircraft, but until you go out and fly it and experience the improved performance, seeing is believing. We're thrilled with the aircraft, and we're pleased we ordered more."

UPS Airlines took delivery of its 28th and final Boeing 747-8 freighter, registration N633UP (c/n 65774), on April 9, 2022.

ABOVE: The 747-8F has 46 cargo positions on its main and lower decks, with 30,288ft³ (857m³) total cargo volume. (Boeing)

BELOW: The same ground handling and cargo loading equipment is used for the 747-8F as the 747-400F to maximise commonality between the two generations. (Boeing)

Converting Airliners to Freighters

An overview of the types of aircraft being re-purposed and converted to freighter aircraft.

Air cargo was growing before COVID-19 struck, but urgent needs for medical supplies globally due to the pandemic and then surging e-commerce demand during the worldwide lockdowns took it to a whole new level.

In early February, the International Air Transport Association (IATA) reported that full-year air cargo demand (measured by cargo tonne/kilometres) was down 8% in 2022 compared to 2021. Released in February 2023, IATA's latest air cargo market figures revealed that global demand was 15.3% below

2021 levels (-15.8% for international operations).

Capacity in 2022, measured in available cargo tonne-kilometres (ACTKs), was 3.0% above 2021 (+4.5% for international operations). Compared to 2019 (pre-COVID) levels, capacity declined by 8.2% (-9.0% for international operations).

A computer-generated image of an A321P2F and an A320P2F in the corporate colours of Elbe Flugzeugwerke. (Airbus)

The upper deck cargo hold on Elbe Flugzeugwerke's so-called A321P2F prototype VH-UHL.
(Elbe Flugzeugwerke)

Monthly cargo demand tracked below 2021 levels from March 2022. Global capacity was 2.2% below 2021 levels (0.5% for international operations). This was the tenth consecutive monthly contraction compared to 2021 performance.

While we may not see the sudden spike of 2019 again, the long term trends for cargo requirements seem to indicate that e-commerce is the new way of the world. And although Airbus and Boeing have both launched new production freighters, the A350F and Boeing 777-8F, passenger-to-freighter or P2F conversions provide a far better indicator of the cargo market, offering as they do a cost-effective route to increasing capacity.

Third-party freighter conversions have been around for years, and while some older airframes have been retired, the plethora of cargo airlines large and small worldwide still uses a sizeable number of converted aircraft such as McDonnell Douglas DC-10s and MD-11s, Boeing 747s/757s/767s and Airbus A300s/A310s.

Mammoth 777 Conversion

Several new projects will add to the number of converted airliners plying their trade through skies. US start-up Mammoth Freighters has its 777-200LRMF/777-300ERMF and Israel Aerospace Industries (IAI) offers the 777-300ERSF 'Big Twin' freighter and the A330-300BDSF. These are the first P2F conversions available for both the 777 and A330.

Mammoth Freighters was founded in December 2020 specifically to develop, build and support 777-200LR/777-300ER conversions. The company's initial 'feedstock' (airframes with ownership/operating costs and flying hours favourable for conversion) comprised ten former Delta Air Lines 777-200LRs. The airframes, each with less than 5,000 cycles since new, were retired by the US legacy carrier in 2020 as part of its COVID-19 cutbacks.

Receipt of its supplemental type certificates from the EASA and the FAA enabled the company and its partners to deliver A321P2F VH-ULD (msn 835), the so-called prototype, to Vallair in September 2020 in the colours of Australia Post for operation by lease customer Qantas.

**An artist's rendering of a Mammoth Freighters'
Boeing 777-200LRMF.** (Mammoth Freighters)

Mammoth announced the Cargojet deal for two initial 777-200LRMF freighters on November 16, 2021. Cargojet holds options for two additional 777-200LRMFs and two 777-300ERMFs.

Mammoth Freighters 777-200LRMF Specifications		
Maximum Take-off Weight (MTOW)	766,000lb	347,452kg
Maximum Landing Weight (MLW)	570,000lb	258,548kg
Max Design Zero Fuel Weight (MZFW)	541,000lb	245,393kg
Operating Empty Weight (OEW)	308,000lb	139,707kg
Max Gross Payload	233,000lb	105,687kg
Total Volume	22,971ft³	650m³
Max Packing Density	10.14 lbs/ft³	162.60 kgs/m³
Maximum Range at Max Payload	4,900nm	4,900nm
Maximum Fuel Capacity	47,890 US Gal	181,283 Lit

Former Delta Air Lines Boeing 777-200LR N705DN (c/n 29742) is the prototype (conformity) article for certification and will be the first aircraft delivered to Cargojet. The aircraft began the conversion process in mid-2022 with test flight scheduled for late 2023 followed by delivery to Cargojet expected in the first quarter of 2024.

Ontario-based Cargojet is Canada's leading provider of time sensitive air cargo services to all major cities across North America, providing dedicated ACMI and International Charter services and carries over 25,000,000lb of cargo weekly. Cargojet operates a network with its own fleet of 31 aircraft.

Mammoth claims its conversions will be "the most productive and economical 777 long-range freighters in the world." Various main deck and lower deck configurations are available. On the 777-200LRMF, the standard 'side-by-side' main deck layout will hold between 15 and 27 contoured pallets or unit load devices (ULDs or containers), with the lower deck compartment having capacity for up to ten pallets or 32 LD3-class containers.

Unsurprisingly, the longer fuselage of the 777-300ER gives the 777-300ERMF variant more capacity – it will have 16 to 33 positions for pallets/ULDs in the main deck 'side-by-side' layout, while the lower hold will carry 14 pallets or 44 LD3s.

A statement from Mammoth Freighters in 2021 said the 777-300ERMF offers 14% more volume than a 747-400F, 81% more than a 767F and 43% more than an MD-11F. Conversion work on the first Mammoth 777 was scheduled to begin in Q2 2022, with supplementary type certification (STC) slated for the second half of 2023.

Mammoth announced AviaAM Leasing (AviaAM) as the launch customer for its 777-300ERMF freighter conversion with an agreement for six aircraft on October 13, 2022. AviaAM is an aviation holding

company that provides tailored aircraft leasing and trading services. The first Avia 777-300ER, conformity aircraft is in work and preparing for a series of pre-modification test flights.

At the time of the AviaAM agreement, Mammoth had firm orders for 29 777 freighter conversions distributed across multiple customers. Additional orders now confirmed by Mammoth exceed 35 aircraft conversions.

The first and conformity 777-300ER of the AviaAM order entered the conversion process in March 2023 at Aspire MRO's state-of-the-art facility at Alliance Airport in Fort Worth, Texas. The Aspire MRO site is being prepared for five 777 conversion lines.

On October 16, 2022, Mammoth announced it had signed a General Terms Agreement with STS Aviation Services (STS) to perform conversions and is planning two production lines. Under the agreement, all work will be accomplished at the STS facility in Manchester, England. The multi-year agreement covers both the 777-200LR and 777-300ER aircraft. The STS facility in Manchester will also provide Mammoth with AOG, product support, and spares provisioning throughout Europe. STS acquired the Manchester facility in early 2022 as part of its expansion efforts. Mammoth expects to induct the first 777 aircraft for modification at the facility in mid-2024.

An artist's rendering of a Mammoth Freighters' Boeing 777-200LRMF and a Boeing 777-300ERMF. (Mammoth Freighters)

Big Twin Freighter

Israel Aerospace Industries (IAI) has undertaken conversions on 737s, 747s and 767s for decades. To date, the firm has converted more than 250 former airliners to 'freight dogs'. Jets converted by the company, redesignated as 737BDSFs, 747BDSFs, and 767BDSFs respectively, are operated by many major cargo operators, including DHL, UPS, and Amazon Prime Air.

IAI launched the 777-300ERSF 'Big Twin' freighter – its name a direct reference to the 'big twin' moniker often used in reference to the 777-300ER – in 2019. Boasting 47 ULD positions on the main deck, IAI says the aircraft will burn 21% less fuel per tonne than the 747-400F and offer 25% more volume than Boeing's own current-production 777-200F.

The company also noted that it will have "the flexibility to be more profitable than the competition at high or low utilisation models" and have "the range capability to seamlessly replace ageing 747-400 and MD-11 freighters."

The first 777-300ERSF conversion (N557CC, formerly A6-EBB with Emirates) entered IAI's Tel Aviv facility in June 2021 following 'pre-conversion preparation'. As IAI has noted: "A new passenger-to-freighter conversion programme requires significant planning and preparation before modifications get underway. Obtaining the supplementary type certificate requires satisfying stringent requirements of civil aviation authorities."

In October 2021, the firm took a key step – cutting a 7m opening across approximately one-third of the aircraft's circumference to install the cargo door. Once the modification work is completed and the 777-300ERSF receives its STC, the aircraft will be delivered to Irish American lessor GE Capital Aviation Services (GECAS), who in turn will lease it to launch operator Kalitta Air. GECAS has ordered 15 777-300ERSFs, with rights on another 15 options.

During the 2021 Dubai Airshow, IAI unveiled Emirates as another 'Big Twin' freighter customer. The Gulf carrier has signed for four conversions to be completed at Etihad Engineering's

IAI B777-300ERSF Big Twin Cargo Conversion Specifications

MTW	777,000lb (35,2441kg)
MTOW	775,000lb (351,534kg)
MZFW	558,000lb (253,104kg)
MLW	583,000lb (264,444kg)
Payload*	222,000lb (100,698kg)
Fuel Capacity	47,890 US Gal (181,283 Lit)
Main Deck Cargo Volume	28,936 ft³ (819m³)
Lower Decks Bulk Volume	600 ft³ (17m³)

* Pending basic aircraft configuration

Main Deck Loading Configurations
Size code A
(32) ULDs 88" x l25" (side by side) plus (1) ULD 88" x l25" (laterally)

Size code B (Military)
(42) ULDs 88" x l08"

Size code B CRAF programme (Military)
(36) ULDs 88" x l08" (side by side) plus (1) ULD 88" x l08" (laterally)

Size code M
(32) ULDs 96" x l25" (side by side) plus (1) ULD 96" x l25" (laterally)

Size code G
(13) ULDs 96" x 238.5" plus (6) ULDs 96" x l25" plus (1) ULD 96" x l25" (laterally)

Size code R
(21) ULDs 96" x l96" (laterally)

Size code G Centreline
(11) ULDs 96" x 238.5" plus (4) ULDs 96" x l25" plus (1) ULD 96" x l25" (laterally)

maintenance, repair, and overhaul (MRO) centre in Abu Dhabi. Conversion work was expected to begin early in 2023.

A330 Conversions

Another new IAI widebody airliner conversion project is the A330-300BDSF. Announced in October 2021, Dublin-based lessor Avolon placed a launch order for 30 jets, with delivery slots from 2025 to 2028. The A330-300 will have 27 ULD/pallet positions.

An IAI statement explained: "IAI's A330-300 conversion includes a low-weight cargo loading system that, by design, reduces related maintenance costs. The Z-shaped rigid barrier provides an additional area forward of the main deck cargo door that can accommodate a ULD or be used to host a crew rest module."

According to IAI, the A330-300BDSF will burn 30% less fuel and offer 30% more volume and 30% more payload than a previous-generation A300/A310, with up to 26 main deck and 32 lower deck positions.

There is also an A330 P2F conversion for both the -200 and -300 variants available from Elbe Flugzeugwerke GmbH (EFW), a joint venture between Airbus and Singapore-based ST Aerospace. Based on the company's earlier A300/A310P2F programme, under which almost 200 aircraft were repurposed as freighters, EFW's A330 conversion offers a 30% increase in volume and payload at 20% lower fuel burn.

Mammoth Freighters 777-300ERMF Specifications		
Maximum Take-off Weight (MTOW)	775,000lb	351,534kg
Maximum Landing Weight (MLW)	572,000lb	259,455kg
Max Design Zero Fuel Weight (MZFW)	543,000lb	246,301kg
Operating Empty Weight (OEW)	323,000lb	146,511kg
Max Gross Payload	220,000lb	99,790kg
Total Volume	28,739ft³	814m³
Max Packing Density	7.7 lbs/ft³	122.59 kgs/m³
Maximum Range at Max Payload	4,800nm	4,800nm
Maximum Fuel Capacity	47,890 US Gal	181,283 Lit

DHL Express was the first EFW A330-300P2F operator in 2017. Eleven examples are now operated by the various carriers who fly for world-leading German logistics company DHL, including European Air Transport Leipzig, ASL Ireland, Air Hong Kong and DHL Air UK.

A330P2F

In 2012, a co-operative venture was announced between Airbus, ST Aerospace in Singapore and Dresden-based EFW, covering conversions of legacy A330-200s and A330-300s. The agreement involved ST Aerospace leading engineering development and EFW leading the industrial phase, with Airbus providing support.

The first two conversions were A330-300P2Fs for DHL Express, which ordered eight examples (with options on ten more). EgyptAir Cargo was the launch customer for the A330-200P2F. One A330-300P2F for DHL was converted by EFW in Dresden and the other in Singapore;

both were delivered to DHL by the end of 2017. This was later than initially planned, as when the A330P2F was launched the target was delivery of the first aircraft in 2016.

Of the two models Airbus says: "The A330-300P2F is designed to be suitable for integrators and express carriers, thanks to its high volumetric payload capability with lower-density cargo. Meanwhile, the A330-200P2F will be optimised for higher-density freight and longer-range performance."

According to EFW, the A330-300P2F carries up to 61,000kg (134,500lb) with a 526m³ (18,581ft³) volume, providing capacity for 26-unit load devices (ULDs) each measuring 96 x 125in (2.4 x 3.1m) or 26 main deck ULDs each measuring 88 x 125in (2.2 x 3.1m). On the lower deck, the aircraft will carry 32 LD3s or nine 96 x 125in ULDs and two 88 x 125in ULDs.

The A330-200P2F carries up to 60,000kg (132,300lb) and has 453m³ (16,016ft³) of volume. Its main deck capacity is 22 ULDs each measuring 96 x 125in or 23

Aspire's MRO Facility at Fort Worth-Alliance Airport, Texas. (Mammoth Freighters)

IAI Bedek's Boeing 777-300ERSF.
(Israel Aerospace Industries)

ULDs measuring 88 x 125in, with 26 lower deck LD3s (or eight 96 x 125in ULDs and two LD3s).

EFW says the A330P2Fs has up to 30% more volume while using up to 20% less fuel per tonne of payload compared to the A300-600P2F, which the A330P2F is designed to replace.

The conversion work involves installing a Class E cargo compartment and linings, window plugs, a main-deck cargo door on the left-hand side of the fuselage, a new reinforced floor grid and panels, a cargo loading system, a 9g barrier net, smoke curtain, door surround structures and a courier area. The conversion also deactivates doors two, three and four, installs new smoke detection and air distribution systems, and upgrades water and waste systems, hydraulics, and lighting.

Conversion

Understandably, repurposing a passenger airliner into a cargo aircraft involves a significant amount of engineering work.

Modification begins with cutting out a section of the fuselage for the hydraulically actuated main deck cargo door and installing a reinforced cargo door surround structure. Fuselage doors (apart from the first pair at the front of the aircraft) are deactivated and mechanically locked, while 'plugs' are placed onto the window cut-outs to seal the fuselage. A rigid cargo barrier is installed with a sliding door to provide access to the cargo compartment from the cockpit.

On larger aircraft, such as a 777 or an A330, an additional compartment may be installed behind the cockpit with supernumerary seats. Depending on the

specific provider and conversion, this may include further amenities such as a crew rest area with bunks, galley and lavatory or an optional configuration for nine economy class seats.

The aircraft will have its original passenger floor structure replaced and/or partially reinforced by stronger crossbeams or panels to support a cargo loading system – including provision for powered and unpowered loading.

Fire protection, air distribution, water/waste, hydraulics, and lighting systems are all upgraded, resulting in extensive work to modify ducting and electrical cabling. A main deck temperature control system is also fitted to allow for the carriage of perishable goods and live animals, while the flight deck computer is upgraded.

In March 2022, airfreight leasing specialist Air Transport Services Group ordered 29 A330P2Fs from EFW for delivery between 2023 and 2027. The conversions will be predominantly undertaken at EFW's facility in Dresden,

but also at ST Engineering sites across China, allowing multiple conversions to occur in parallel.

In April 2022, for the first time since launching the A330P2F programme, EFW delivered a pair of converted jets within just four weeks of each other: A330-300P2F EI-GVZ to CDB Aviation and A330-200P2F EI-MYY to Altavair, both of which will be leased to Mexican cargo carrier MAS.

Boeing 757s and 767s

Despite the presence of 777 and A330 conversions, an October 2021 IBA consultancy analysis pointed out that demand "remains very strong" for earlier aircraft, including Boeing's 767 and 757.

While Boeing has its in-house 767-300BCF (Boeing Converted Freighter), which the aerospace giant says offers 18% better fuel efficiency than the A330, IAI offers its 767-200/300BDSF. ABX Air, Air Transport International (ATI), Amerijet International, Atlas Air, Cargojet Airways, the various carriers flying for DHL, FedEx Express, Omni Air International and UPS Airlines are among those operating converted 767s, with many of the ATI and Atlas Air jets being operated on behalf of Amazon Prime Air.

Similarly, numerous ex-passenger 757s – including the last few examples retired by British charter airline TUI in late 2021 – have undergone freighter conversion. As with the 767, key operators include large cargo players such as DHL, UPS Airlines and China's SF Airlines.

767 Conversions

A direct competitor for the A330P2F in the midsize market segment is the

IAI Bedek's Boeing 777-300ERSF
'Big Twin' showing the aft cargo door
open. (Israel Aerospace Industries)

IAI A330-300BDSF Cargo Conversion Specifications

MTW	515,700lb (233,918kg)
MTOW*	513,677; 518,086; 533,519lb (233,000kg; 235,000kg; 242,000kg)
MZFW	385,809lb (175,000kg)
MLW	412,264Ib (187,000kg)
Payload	134,500lb (61,008kg)
Fuel Capacity*	25,765 - 37,744 US Gal (97,531 – 142,877 Lit)
Main Deck Cargo Volume	15,063ft³ (427m³)
Lower Decks Bulk Volume	4,018ft³ (114m³)
Bulk Cargo Usable Volume	649ft³ (18m³)

* Pending basic aircraft configuration

Main Deck Loading Configurations*

* With Z shaped 9G rigid barrier, allowing an additional ULD position with cargo volume increase up to 500 ft³

Size Code M
27 96" x l25" ULDs
Size Code A
27 88" x l25" ULDs
Size Code B
30 88" x 108" ULDs
463L (Military)
30 88" x l08" ULDs
Size Code M (Centreline)
18 96" x l25" ULDs
Size Code A (Centreline)
20 88" x l25" ULDs
Size Code M (Longitudinal, Centreline)]
16 96" x l25" ULDs
Size Code R (Centreline)
Four 16ft ULDs plus 13 96" x l25" ULDs
Size Code G (Centreline)
Four 20ft ULDs plus 11 96" x l25" ULDs

converted Boeing 767-300/767-300ER. There are currently two conversion options for this aircraft: Boeing's own 767-300BCF (Boeing Converted Freighter) and the 767-300BDSF (Bedek Special Freighter) conversion offered under a supplemental type certificate (STC) by IAI Bedek, the maintenance, repair, and overhaul arm of Israel Aerospace Industries.

Boeing's 767-300BCF has 24 positions for 88 x 125in ULDs on the main deck and can lift approximately 114,500lb (51,930kg) of payload. IAI Bedek's 767-300BDSF also offers 24 main-deck positions for 88 x 125in ULDs. The Israeli company's product offers a total structural payload of 125,200lb (56,699kg) for winglet-equipped aircraft or 128,200lb (58,150kg) for those without winglets.

The 767-300BDSF complements IAI Bedek's other 767 P2F conversion, the 767-200BDSF for 767-200s/767-200ERs, which carries a typical load of 19 88 x 125in ULDs and offers a maximum take-off weight of up to 351,000lb (159,210kg).

A 767-300BDSF features a new cargo lining and ceiling, a cargo loading system, a 9g rigid barrier, a main deck cargo door and structure, reinforced frames, replacement floor beams, new seat tracks, floor panels and drain system, aluminium window plugs, three supernumerary seats, and a new galley and lavatory.

The 767-300BDSF/767-200BDSF conversions are conducted by Bedek in Tel Aviv. The 767-300BCF work is undertaken by ST Aerospace in Singapore and, from 2018, by Evergreen Aviation Technologies Corporation in Taiwan, which previously converted three 747-400Fs into the 747-400LCFs used to transport 787 fuselage subassemblies to the Dreamliner assembly lines.

Airbus A320 and A321P2F

Conversions do not just involve large airliners, with air cargo's recent rise having really been supercharged by countless Airbus A320 and Boeing 737 conversions. A significant recent development in this segment of the P2F conversion market was the European Union Aviation Safety Agency (EASA) issuing EFW's A320P2F conversion with its STC in March 2022.

An EFW statement said: "The A320P2F can accommodate ten container and one pallet positions in the main deck, with seven container positions in the lower deck. Given its gross payload of up to 21 tonnes at a maximum range of 1,850nm and total usable containerised volume of 159m³, the freighter aircraft has 85% stowage efficiency. This makes the A320P2F an ideal freighter platform to serve the fast-growing e-commerce market globally."

The A320P2F is EFW's second Airbus narrowbody P2F solution after the A321P2F, which was certified by EASA

(Israel Aerospace Industries)

and delivered to initial operator Qantas in 2019.

Airbus A320P2F and A321P2F

Elbe Flugzeugwerke based in Dresden, Germany, ST Engineering in Singapore, and Airbus are currently working on A320P2F and A321P2F conversions. Both programmes were originally launched at the 2015 Paris Air Show.

The A320P2F has 11 main-deck Unit Load Device (ULD) positions and carries 21,000kg (46,300lb) of payload over 2,100nm (3,889km) and the larger A321P2F has 14 main-deck ULD positions, carries a 27,000kg (59,500lb) payload and a range of 1,900nm (3,158km) range.

A P2F conversion includes the installation of an extra-large, hydraulically actuated, and electrically locked main cargo door on the forward fuselage, a Class E main deck cargo compartment, a full rigid 9g cargo/smoke barrier with a sliding door, window plugs, a replaced and reinforced floor grid, new freighter floor panels, main deck cargo linings and ceilings.

Doors 2R, 3L, 3R, 4L and 4R are deactivated and mechanically locked and, like the A330P2F, there is upgraded hydraulic, fire protection, lighting, and air distribution. A revised flight deck

(Israel Aerospace Industries)

includes the cockpit, supernumerary seats, and a new lavatory.

Airbus says advantages of the A320P2F and A321P2F include compatibility with the A330P2F, enabling crews to move across fleets and mixed-fleet flying.

Market Trends

In short, there's a lot of activity in the conversions market because a couple of trends are coalescing. First, and despite the choppy state of the air cargo market in recent years, the continued increase in e-commerce, not least by Amazon's seemingly never-ending expansion. Second, a growing feedstock of aircraft reaching the end of their service lives as passenger airliners is also driving the P2F market. A point has been reached in the product life cycle of these aircraft where their residual values have fallen to the level that it is cost-effective for asset owners to convert them to freighters.

These background factors are set to keep the P2F conversions market buoyant well into the future, according to

the manufacturers. Airbus' latest Global Market Forecast envisages a requirement for 1,550 conversions over a 20-year period through 2041.

With this long-term potential it is little wonder there are set to be further developments in the market.

Saxon-Asian Freighter

On February 7, 2018, in Dresden, Germany, Elbe Flugzeugwerke (EFW) and its joint venture partners ST Engineering and Airbus announced Vallair Solutions Sàrl (Vallair) as its launch customer for its A321P2F passenger-to-freighter conversion. The French company has committed to 10 A321P2F freighter conversions, each to a 14-pallet cargo configuration. According to EFW the A321P2F is the first in its size category to offer containerised loading in both the main deck (up to 14 container positions) and lower deck (up to 10 container positions). The jet's payload-range capability of 62,000lb over 2,300nm is described by EFW

as "generous", and ideal for express domestic and regional operations. Each A321P2F features optimised weight distribution to enable empty flights and random loading, and provides flexibility for operators, in particular express carriers.

At the time of the announcement Gregoire Lebigot, president and CEO of Vallair said: "We see a huge potential in the A321P2F, not only as a replacement of the Boeing 757F, but as a key tool for the cargo industry to achieve the projected growth rate of the air freight market in general – driven by express services and e-commerce. The A321P2F will be the first aircraft to introduce a containerised lower deck to the market segment of narrow body freighters: a significant game changer for any hub and spoke operation."

The prototype A321P2F made its post-conversion first flight on January 22, 2020, from ST Engineering's facility at Seletar airport in Singapore. The aircraft subsequently completed a series of flight tests in support of gaining the type's

A Boeing 767BDSF under conversion at IAI's Bedek facility. (Israel Aerospace Industries)

supplemental type certificate (STC) from the European Union Aviation Safety Agency (EASA).

Certification quickly followed, the EASA issued the notification to EFW (the STC holder) on February 24, just a month after the prototype made its first flight. In addition to holding the STC, EFW has many responsibilities for the A321P2F programme including adaption engineering in the serial phase, subcontracting of work to each conversion line, overall programme management, customer support services, and marketing and sales. EFW describes its P2F programme as "exclusive, whereby Airbus contributes with OEM data and certification support."

The OEM support helps to preserve lifecycle value, given its superiority in quality, reliability, and ease of maintenance.

Lim Serh Ghee, President of ST Engineering said: "The swift process in attaining EASA's STC shortly after the first flight test is a testament to the engineering and design strengths of our P2F solution."

In late July, EFW received an STC for the A321P2F issued by the Federal Aviation Administration. Customer specific requirements were subsequently integrated into the aircraft and certified prior to its re-delivery.

Receipt of the STC enabled the company and its partners to deliver the first A321P2F jet converted, VH-ULD (msn 835), the so-called prototype, to Vallair in September in the colours of Australia Post for operation by lease customer Qantas. The aircraft entered service on October 27, 2020.

Mr Jeffrey Lam, president of ST Engineering's aerospace sector, said, "With the A321P2F platform being the best-in-class for its size category – having 55% more volumetric capacity than its nearest competitor – we are confident that the programme will be a great success in the freighter market."

The next customer delivery took place on January 7, 2021, when the first A321P2F for aircraft lease management company, BBAM Limited Partnership was handed over. The jet was bound for its lease customer, British charter airline, Titan Airways.

Commenting on the delivery, Alastair Willson, managing director of Titan said: "The A321P2F will enable us to utilise all the benefits of this type into our air freight activities including best-in-class economics, reduced noise, a lower carbon footprint and real time health monitoring, ensuring the highest levels of reliability."

BBAM signed a general terms agreement in December 2019 for several A321P2F conversions, the first of which entered the programme at ST Engineering's Seletar facility in January 2020.

EFW's P2F conversion programme evolved in the spring of 2021 when ST Engineering entered the first A320 into the P2F programme at its Seletar facility with 25,159 cycles and 40,376 hours on the clock. This was the world's first ever A320P2F conversion.

ST Engineering subsequently set up new conversion lines in Singapore, Guangzhou, China and Brookley Field in Mobile, Alabama to ramp-up the number of conversion slots to 23 per year in a bid to meet market demand.

On May 6, 2021 EFW announced an order for four Airbus A321P2F conversions placed by Dublin-based leasing company GTLK Europe, a new customer to EFW. Three A321s entered the conversion programme in 2021, the fourth followed in 2022.

American Freighter

In August 2017, Precision Aircraft Solutions and Air Transport Services Group (ATSG) announced the formation of 321 Precision Conversions, a joint-venture company, to develop a P2F conversion of Airbus A321-200 aircraft.

Precision Aircraft Solutions started full-scale engineering for STC development during Q3 2016. At the time of the announcement 321 Precision Conversions anticipated approval of a supplemental type certificate (STC) for A321-200 conversions in 2019.

Unsurprisingly, 321 Precision Conversions said its A321-200 freighter would provide a best-in-class solution, which would fulfil both replacement and growth needs in the narrowbody freighter market, "it will deliver cube space

commensurate to Boeing 757 freighters, and low operating costs comparable to smaller Boeing 737 freighters, making it an attractive platform for air express network operators."

Dubbed the A321-200PCF, 321 Precision Conversions' freighter features.

- 14 A-code 88 x 125in positions
- Cargo volume 7,963ft^3
- Containerised volume 7,280ft^3
- Standard payload of approximately 59,680lb
- Retention of full size L1/R1 doors
- TELAIR main deck cargo loading system
- A lower compartment below the main deck compatible with bulk, sliding carpet, or containerised systems
- Loading flexibility with dual locks for PAG-type netted pallets or two AKH containers at the 14th position
- Crew galley with baggage stowage
- Full size lavatory

On October 10, 2020, the company's first converted A321-200 freighter made its maiden flight at Orlando-Sanford International Airport, Florida following its conversion by Avocet MRO Services at the airport.

After the flight, 321 Precision Conversions president Gary Warner said: "This milestone flight was nominal in all respects, with all primary and secondary

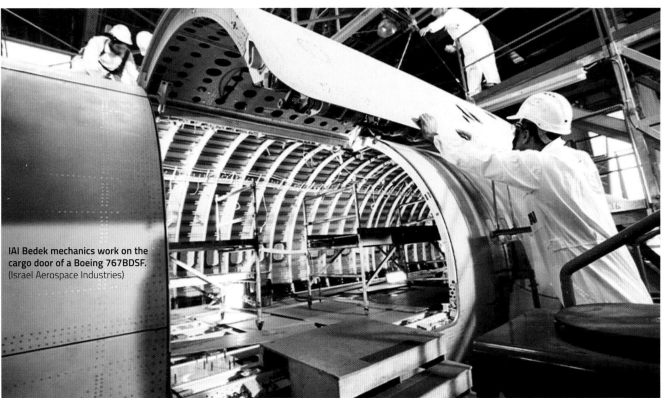

IAI Bedek mechanics work on the cargo door of a Boeing 767BDSF.
(Israel Aerospace Industries)

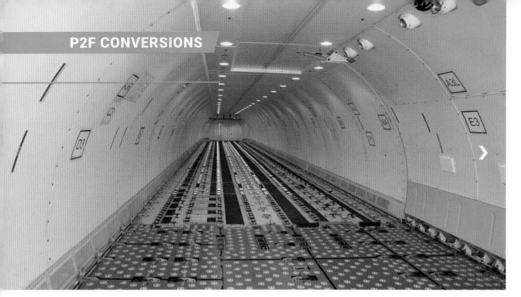

The cargo bay of a Boeing 767-200BDSF features a new cargo lining and ceiling, replacement floor beams, new seat tracks, floor panels and drain system, and aluminium window plugs.
(Israel Aerospace Industries)

systems - including the cargo door and supporting sub-systems, functioning perfectly as designed. Based on the results of this maintenance test flight – a prerequisite prior to entering certification flight testing – we look forward to a brisk progression to full certification."

321 Precision Conversions received FAA approval of a supplemental type certificate (STC) for its A321-200PCF in April 2021.

On June 29, 2021, Wilmington, Ohio-based ATSG announced a commitment by its leasing business, Cargo Aircraft Management, to purchase two Airbus A321-200s for conversion to freighter configuration at the company's PEMCO Conversions facilities in Tampa, Florida.

On March 8, 2022, ATSG announced that PEMCO Conversions, a division of wholly owned ATSG subsidiary Pemco World Air Services, inducted its first Airbus A321 aircraft for the A321-200PCF freighter conversion developed by 321.

At the time of the announcement Mike Berger, ATSG's chief commercial officer said: "We have accelerated our plans to invest in and offer this midsize, mid-range freighter type because our express-network customers have expressed strong interest in adding it to their fleets. Since the development of our passenger-to-freighter conversion design for the A321-200 commenced in 2017, it was with the intention to extend our leased-freighter options into this airframe type in the future. It is very well suited for air-express service and e-commerce fulfilment over shorter routes and with smaller payloads as a complement to our existing fleet of more than 85 larger Boeing 767 converted freighters, and with better performance than Boeing 757 freighters or any Boeing 737 freighter variants. The time is right to launch this milestone

initiative for ATSG and its aircraft leasing customers."

The A321-200PCF delivers the highest available payload with unmatched versatility, offering the flexible TELAIR main deck cargo loading system and a lower lobe compatible with bulk, sliding carpet, or containerised systems. It has an operating empty weight over 2,000lb lighter than its closest rival and has been optimised for maximum revenue loads, profitability, fuel efficiency, and room for supernumeraries.

At the time of the aircraft's induction, Berger said: "The A321-200PCF is very well suited for global air-express service and e-commerce fulfilment over shorter routes. It combines next generation efficiency with best-in-platform cargo capacity, crew amenities, and efficiency. It represents an opportunity for Boeing 757 operators to modernise their fleet, offering, for example, a 13% improvement in fuel efficiency over a Boeing 757-200 series freighter. Additionally, switching to the A321-200PCF allows operators of the Boeing 737-800 to expand their air cargo capacity to meet additional market demand."

Cargo Aircraft Management's first A321-200PCF conversions are being conducted under a letter of intent from Malaysia-based Raya Airways, which provides air cargo service to more than ten locations across the Asia-Pacific region.

The two aircraft to be converted are former Thomas Cook Airlines UK machines, registrations G-TCDV (msn 1972) and G-TCDX (msn 1887). In early March 2023, both aircraft were still undergoing conversion.

As a follow-on, Raya Airways plans to lease additional A320 Family converted freighters from ST Engineering's asset management business: two A320P2Fs and two A321P2Fs. The four aircraft will undergo conversion with Elbe

Flugzeugwerke (EFW), the first is former Sky Angkor Airlines A321-200, registration XU-707 (msn 1293).

First A321P2F Enters Service

After nearly two years of work, A321P2F VH-ULD (msn 835) was delivered to launch operator Qantas for use on behalf of Australia Post. The conversion was completed by Elbe Flugzeugwerke (EFW), a joint venture created by Airbus and ST Engineering. The new P2F version is being leased to Express Freighters Australia – a wholly-owned subsidiary of Qantas Freight – by aircraft asset manager Vallair.

Andreas Hermann, VP asset management at Airbus and member of the EFW shareholder committee said: "The Airbus A321 is the platform which, by design, will offer the best economics, cargo capacity and performance in the single-aisle freighter segment going forward. For any asset owner, this will provide an excellent opportunity to leverage future growth and replacement waves, underpinning the already great value proposition of the A321 today."

The aptly registered aircraft – ULD being a unit load device – is a former British Midland example that was delivered to the Castle Donington-based carrier on June 12, 1998. Since then, it served with Air 2000, bmi British Midland, Turkey's Onur Air, and Iraq-based Zagrosjet.

Airbus says the type is the first in its size category to offer containerised loading in both the main (up to 14 full positions) and lower deck (up to 10 locations). With a payload-range capability that can carry 28 tonnes over 2,300nm (4,260km), the A321P2F is well positioned for express domestic and regional operations.

The conversion features a large main cargo door which is hydraulically actuated and electrically locked, a Class-E main-deck cargo compartment with full rigid 9g barrier for optimal protection between crew and cargo, and a redefined flight deck that includes supernumerary seats.

Vallair's narrowbody freight conversion programme gained plenty of interest from well-established and forward-looking cargo operators worldwide. A lease agreement with SmartLynx Malta for two newly converted A321-200 freighters was signed on October 15, 2020. Six days later, the lessor announced a deal with Miami-based Global Crossing Airlines or GlobalX, for the lease of ten A321F conversions which were slated for delivery by Q2 2023.

E-Jet Freighters

Brazilian multinational aerospace giant Embraer recently launched a freighter conversion programme for its successful E190 and E195 narrowbody regional jets. Pledging 'head-turning performance and economics', Embraer said: "Overhead bins are removed, there are new smoke detection and fire suppression systems, the main-deck floor is reinforced and has a cargo handling system, and there is a new forward cargo door."

The converted E190F will have a 23,608lb total payload and carry seven ULD pallets on the main deck and underfloor, while the E195F offers a 27,112lb payload and can carry eight ULDs. Embraer says the E195F will have similar range and payload to the Boeing 737-300SF, but consumes "less fuel, generates fewer emissions, and [has] lower maintenance and cash operating costs".

The conversions will bring "right-sizing to the cargo industry by tapping the gap between turboprop and larger narrowbody freighters," the manufacturer claimed.

With the firm forecasting demand for around 700 aircraft of this size over the next 20 years, the president, and CEO of Embraer Commercial Aviation, Arjan Meijer, said the huge appetite for cargo aircraft had been a key factor in the timing of the project.

Although initial deliveries are planned for 2024, no customers have been announced.

According to EFW's sales director, Thomas Centner: "The strength of the A321 is its capability to accommodate fully containerised cargo on both decks – a game-changer in this freighter size segment and something which is not available on competing freighter platforms up to the 757." The A320P2F offers 14 main deck and ten lower deck positions. According to Centner: "Using containers avoids the risk of damage caused by hand-loading – something which cargo airlines want to avoid if possible. The competing 737 freighter can only offer container positions on the main deck and bulk cargo on the lower holds. Furthermore, access to the 737's lower hold is constrained due to its smaller and inward-opening doors."

Boeing 737 Conversions

Various conversion options are available for 737s. Boeing launched its own inhouse -800BCF conversion for the widely operated 800-series in 2016. It is designed to carry up to 52,800lb on 2,023nm routes and 12 main deck ULDs.

Following US Federal Aviation Administration certification, the first converted jet – the 2004-vintage N346PH for lessor GECAS – was re-registered G-NPTA and delivered to West Atlantic at East Midlands Airport in 2018. ASL Airlines, China Postal Airlines and Tianjin Air Cargo are among other carriers that have since introduced the -800BCF into service.

Miami, Florida-based Aeronautical Engineers Inc (AEI) holds various STCs for 737 family aircraft, with its converted jets re-designated as 737SFs. Capacity on its options range from seven ULDs and a 37,800lb payload on the -300SF to 11 containers and a 52,700lb payload on for the -800SF.

Another 737-800 P2F conversion is offered by IAI, with the 737-800BDSF available in three different configuration options for ULDs and pallets. The Israeli company also offers three separate configuration options for the 737-700.

Tampa, Florida-based PEMCO Conversions offers a nine-pallet and 'quick-change' conversions for the 737-300 Classic, along with full-freighter and 'combi' layouts for the 737-700.

Boeing 737-800

In 2018, Boeing will deliver its first 737-800BCF, which since its February 2016 launch has secured 30 firm orders and 25 commitments, mainly from Chinese carriers, including YTO Airlines and China Postal Airlines. The conversions will take place at Boeing Shanghai Aviation Services and STAECO in Jinan.

The 737-800BCF is designed to carry up to 52,800lb (23,949kg) of cargo on 2,023 nautical mile (3,750km) routes. The aircraft has 12 ULD positions, with 5,000ft³ (141.5m³) of cargo space on the main deck. There is a further 1,540ft³ (43.7m³) of capacity in two lower-lobe compartments. Modifications required to convert a 737-800 into a freighter include installing a large main-deck cargo door, a cargo-handling system and accommodation for up to four non-flying crew members or passengers.

Boeing Commercial Airplane's regional director of product marketing, George Alabí said: "[The 737-800BCF] offers freighter operators newer technology, lower fuel consumption and better reliability." Its higher payload capability and longer range compared to a converted 737 Classic will, he said, improve cargo operators' ability to open new markets.

Boeing's 737-800BCF conversion provides competition for two separate third-party products from AEI and IAI Bedek, which both hold STCs to convert 737-800s.

Miami-based AEI announced its 737-800SF programme in 2015. The company's product sits alongside its other STCs for 737 Classics: an 11-pallet conversion for the 737-400, ten-pallet and nine-pallet conversions for the 737-300 and an eight-pallet option for the 737-200. AEI also offers eight-pallet and 12-pallet conversions for the Bombardier CRJ200 and the MD-80, respectively.

The AEI 737-800SF conversion will install an 86 x 140in (2.1 x 3.5m) cargo door on the left side of the fuselage and modify the main deck to a Class E cargo compartment able to carry 11 88 x 125in ULD and up to five supernumerary seats. Compared to the 52,800lb payload capability of Boeing's in-house 737-800BCF, the AEI 737-800SF will offer a 52,000lb (23,587kg) main deck payload.

Boeing launched its 737-800BCF conversion for the 737-800 in 2016, with the conversion providing competition for AEI's 737-800SF and IAI Bedek's 737-800BDSF. (Boeing)

The cargo door will be hydraulically operated and actuated from the inside of the aircraft by an independent system using hydraulic pressure drawn from either an electrically operated hydraulic pump or a manual hand pump. There will be a reinforced floor, a single vent door system, cabin windows replaced with lightweight aluminium window plugs, a 9g rigid cargo/smoke barrier with a sliding door, a relocated digital flight data recorder enabling an 84.5in (2.1m) ceiling height throughout the cargo compartment and stretch-formed fuselage skins.

The IAI Bedek 737-800 P2F conversion is the 737-800BDSF, which offers three different configuration options: 11 88 x 125in ULDs and one 79 x 60.4in (2 x 1.5m) ULD; 11 88 x 108in ULDs and one 79 x 60.4in ULD; or nine 88 x 125in ULDs and one smaller ULD and a single pallet. The brochure for the 737-800BDSF quotes a 53,000lb (20,040kg) payload.

The first 737-800SF was delivered by AEI to the conversion's launch customer, GECAS, in early 2019. The lessor has ordered 20 conversions from AEI, and it is also the launch customer for Boeing's 737-800BCF. The initial 737-800SF, last operated by Corendon Airlines in Turkey, was handed over by GECAS to AEI in Miami in May 2016. Altogether, AEI has secured 80 orders for the 12-pallet 737-800SF. The first aircraft from an agreement with an undisclosed customer, covering 15 aircraft plus 15 options, was due to start conversion in 2018 for delivery in 2019.

Supply and Demand

While the availability of multiple P2F options is striking, it is the number of ongoing conversions that provides the most telling symbol of air cargo's growth. Just taking the 737-800 conversions as an example, Boeing reported in November 2021 that it had secured more than 200 orders and commitments from 19 customers for its 737-800BCF in just five years.

Conversion capabilities are also expanding. From 2022, Boeing will be opening new 737-800BCF facilities at its London-Gatwick MRO facility, KF Aerospace's MRO centre in Kelowna, Canada, and in China.

Meanwhile, an April 2022 statement from EFW said: "To meet the rising demand for freighter conversions, ST Engineering and EFW are setting up new conversion sites in China and the US this year and are ramping up conversion capacity for all their Airbus P2F programmes to over 60 slots per year by 2024." AEI is also expanding its -800SF capabilities with new production lines at KF Aerospace, Commercial Jet Services in Dothan, Alabama, and the HAECO Xiamen and Shandong Aircraft Engineering Company in China.

Aircraft owners use various factors to decide which aircraft are suitable for cargo conversion. Their age, maintenance records and specific ownership, leasing and operating costs are all part of the decision.

A 2021 analysis by industry consultants IBA said the A321P2F has significant potential, including as a replacement for ever-ageing midsize A300 and 757 freighters. IBA noted: "The initial [A321P2F] conversions were focused on late-1990s build aircraft and as the programme has matured, we have seen younger examples [of the jet] enter the fray. As feedstock of 757s dries up eventually, and prices of A321 passenger aircraft come down, we see a whole raft of conversions ahead."

The industry consultants also predict prospects for the A330P2F: "Feedstock pricing of newer aircraft is reducing. Pre-COVID, a 2009 Rolls-Royce-powered A330-300 was a US$25m aircraft – [the] same aircraft [is] now a US$15m asset. This means cargo operators can seek much younger aircraft and reap the benefits of additional years of useful life and a longer-term investment in the asset."

"The A321P2F has significant potential as a replacement for ever-ageing midsize A300 and 757 freighters."

Although the demand for freighters grew during the coronavirus pandemic, a healthy conversions market is predicted over the long term.

In its latest 20-year World Air Cargo Forecast issued in November 2022, Boeing forecast strong demand for air cargo services through 2041, with traffic doubling and the world's freighter fleet expanding by more than 60%, and a requirement for nearly 2,800 freighters, one third of which will consist of new production freighters, while the remaining two-thirds will be freighter conversions.

Brazilian multinational aerospace giant Embraer has launched a freighter conversion programme for its successful E190 and E195 narrowbody regional jets. (Embraer)